JOHN MANUEL LOZANO

Praying Even When the Door Seems Closed

The Nature and Stages of Prayer

PAULIST PRESS   New York/Mahwah

Book design by Ellen Whitney

Library of Congress Cataloging-in-Publication Data

Lozano, Juan M.
    Praying even when the door seems closed: the nature and stages of prayer / by John M. Lozano.
        p.   cm.
    Bibliography: p.
    ISBN 0-8091-3048-3; $6.95 (est.)
    1. Prayer.   2. Spiritual life—Catholic authors.   I. Title.
BV210.2.L69 1989
    248.3'2—dc19   88-29065
                                                            CIP

Published by Paulist Press
997 Macarthur Boulevard
Mahwah, NJ 07430

Printed and bound in the
United States of America

Contents

FOREWORD 1

1 APPROACHING THE THEME 5

Prayer as Conversation 6
Prayer as a Lifting Up 11
At the Very Core: Presence and Relation 13
Prayer and Intimacy 16
Prayer, a Divine Gift 18
Accepting the Gift: Fidelity 21
How St. Teresa of Jesus Understood Prayer 23

2 JESUS AND PRAYER 28

Jesus Prays 28
Filial Relationship 31
More by Example Than by Teaching 33
Prayer and Faith 35
Prayer and God's Will 36
God-Centered Prayer 38

3 PRAYER AND LIFE 40

Prayer as Remembering 43
Prayer as Discovery 44
Prayer as Discernment 45
Praying Within History 46
Praying in the Blood of Christ 49
Prayer from the Heart of the World 52
Prayer at Work 55
Meeting God During the Rush Hour 58
Prayer and Ministry 59

4   THE FIRST THREE DEGREES OF PRAYER   ...   62

The Causes of Progress 64
The Goal 66
Point of Departure: The Word 69
Reciting, Meditating, Feeling 72
The First Degree: The Prayer of Recitation 73
The Second Degree: Meditation 75
The Third Degree: Affective Prayer 80
Christ in the Prayer of His Disciples 82

5   PRAYER AND CRISIS: THE CRISES OF PRAYER   85

The Crises of Prayer 87
The First Tests 87
Prayer of Dryness and Boredom 88
A Dead-End Street 90
Self-Contentment and the Experience of Powerlessness   93
Abandoning Personal Prayer 96

6   WAITING FOR GOD 100

What To Do? 100
Mary and Lazarus 101
Prayer and Hope 103
The Prayer of the Poor 104
Needy Creatures 105
Discretion Is Necessary 106
How To Behave 109
Be Still and Know That I Am God 112
A Most General Way 113

7   APPROACHING MYSTICAL EXPERIENCE 117

A Scholarly Discussion 117
Universal Call 119

Christian Tradition on Mysticism 121
Mystics and Visionaries 123
A Few Examples 127
The Goal of the Life of Prayer 129

8   THE HIGHER DEGREES OF PRAYER 130

Drawn into Oneself 133
The Prayer of Quiet 135
The Prayer of Simple Union 139
Ecstatic Union 140

9   PRAYER IN THE DARK 144

The Night of the Spirit 146
Two Interpretations or Two Modes 147
Nature and Cause 150
The Night and the Cross 152
Prayer in a Limit-Situation 153
The Night of Jesus 156

10   YOU SHALL LOVE THE LORD YOUR GOD WITH
     ALL YOUR HEART 160

The Just Live by Faith 162
Mysticism, Morals and Prophecy 163
Effects 164
Cross and Glory 166
Constant Amazement 167

   NOTES 169

   INDEX 181

To Jeanne Heidemann,
with whom I have shared most of it

Foreword

This book has a rather long history. For some years I have been teaching a class on "Theology and Forms of Prayer." At the same time I have directed a few workshops and even a few retreats precisely on the topic of prayer. Both activities, academic and ministerial, have brought me in contact with a good number of Christians who regularly cultivate personal prayer, as well as with others whose prayer life is virtually besieged by job-related concerns. Of the latter, some appear to be genuinely hungry for the grace of God, while others seem to be haunted by nostalgia for a lost past.

These activities gave me a chance to meet several persons who were simple (in a good sense) of heart and mind, to whom prayer (God bless them!) offered no particular difficulty. But they also led me to discover a much greater number of believers for whom, as for Saint Paul (though in a different sense), prayer was a struggle. In the confidences they shared with me, I noticed that a set of images recurred with some frequency. Many of these people felt that they were standing still in front of a closed door or a high, impenetrable wall. I also began discovering that in their efforts to open such a door or batter down that wall (as if any human power were capable of doing so!), many of them had adopted some erroneous attitudes. Often enough, the reason God "does not come to us" is not because our sins are a rebuff to God's justice, but rather because we, through our mistaken attitudes, don't allow God to get through to us.

This led me to conceive the project of putting my knowledge of Christian tradition, as well as my acquaintance with the spiritual experiences of others that I have been treasuring up over the years, at the service of these harried believers. I hope that both they and God will forgive me for my temerity in attempting to do so.

This explains the title of the book, *Praying Even When the Door Seems Closed*. And, in fact, this is the theme of the central part of the book. But I soon realized that before I could talk about the "long wait" before the closed door, I would have to clarify a number of presuppositions: what prayer is for a Christian, what place prayer holds in our life, and what the first stages of prayer are before we reach this blind alley, the night of the senses that is sometimes prolonged because of our lack of understanding. Then it occurred to me that it would not be out of place to say something about the later stages, those of "contemplation," so that some of these people could see where the Spirit of God wants to lead them (for there's no shortage of the Spirit in our days), while others could have a true picture of the situation they're in. The book deals, then, with prayer and the way of prayer, with particular emphasis on the quite common experience of powerlessness in prayer.

This book seemed destined to be one of those I call *heart books* rather than *head books*. It has been my experience that some of my books have taken shape in my mind as a sort of by-product of academic investigation and reflection, while others have gradually taken shape through a longer and more silent sort of gestation in my heart. In the long run, the latter come more easily to birth. But as I was writing this book with the intention of speaking heart to heart, it dawned on me that it might be well to distill in it something of what Christian tradition has had to say about prayer, translating it into present-day language and life contexts. This is not as common as one might think, because many people who write treatises on spirituality seem to feel obliged to stick to a vocabulary and to points of view that don't mean anything today. Yet it seems that those poor Christians who have not had the fortune to become familiarized with these categories nonetheless feel obliged to enter through them if they want to learn anything about spirituality. I realized, then, that I would have to translate what was best and most enduring in the Christian tradition. I say "the" Christian tradition, and not just that of one school or another, as is commonly done. Some writers stick exclusively to Teresa of Jesus and completely ignore the mysticism of the twelfth century Cistercians, Benedictines and Canons Regular—and vice versa. Other writers limit themselves to the last four centuries, without so much as casting a glance at the extremely rich teaching of the fathers of the church or the wisdom of the fathers and mothers of the desert. I have done my best to broaden these horizons.

I have also carefully tried to keep the intellectual contribution from hindering the heart-to-heart dialogue. Hence, although the book constantly alludes to the experiences and thoughts of the great witnesses of Christian tradition, I have avoided making it an academic book, in order to adhere to my original aim, which was to help others to stay faithful to the gift of prayer. Although I may be mistaken, I would like to think that I have kept a balance between a pious book with no doctrinal meat and an academic study that is too dry to be of help to others.

This book is addressed to the considerable number of Christians who already have some contact with the life of prayer: persons in lay ministries or in prayer groups, religious, seminarians and priests, lay Christians committed to prayer—above all, to those who are struggling.

As far as language is concerned, the reader will note that there has been an effort to use inclusive vocabulary. Along these lines I have avoided using masculine pronouns in referring to God, I have used the noun "reign" instead of "kingdom," and Christ instead of "the Lord." Only in describing Jesus' experience of his abba have I used masculine pronouns in referring to God. In contrast, since the Spirit is feminine and expresses God's femininity in the Hebrew Bible of Jesus, I have used "she" and "her" when speaking of the Spirit.

I would like once more to express my thanks to my collaborator and advisor, the Rev. Josep Daries, for his efforts to put my text in fluent and precise English, and especially for helping me use an inclusive language which, it is hoped, will neither offend nor exclude anyone.

1

Approaching the Theme

Either from our own experience or from what we have seen in others, we have all gathered some idea of what prayer is: putting oneself in the presence of the divinity and establishing some sort of relationship with it. This is how we all pray, whether we be Christians, Jews, Muslims, Hindus, Shintoists or whatever. Naturally, "putting ourselves in the presence of the divinity" means different things to different people. A Greek farmer, a Neopolitan fruit vendor and a Mexican or Ecuadorian Indian simply station themselves before a sacred icon. Theirs is a very unitary world. On the one hand, the supernatural forms part of their daily life and they don't have to escape from it in order to find God. On the other hand, for them, representation and reality are closely linked. But city-folk like us, more-or-less educated and beset by a thousand daily concerns, have to make a conscious effort to withdraw into ourselves in search of silence and what little solitude we can find. In both cases, however, there is that same contact with the mysterious presence of God and that same communication with God. When, as in Buddhism, there is only an inward turning, without contact with a God who calls us and moves us, there is no prayer properly speaking, but something that we might call, in a very special sense, meditation. The Buddhist turns inward in order to find total reality beyond the self.

Prayer as Conversation

One way or another—through the liturgy, or perhaps in catechism class—we have all heard definitions of prayer that have been repeated in Christianity since the third century.

Perhaps the commonest of these definitions is the one that understands prayer as a conversation with the divinity. The Bible itself suggests this notion when it tells us that God used to speak with Moses face to face (Nm 12:6–8). One doesn't have to be an expert in exegesis to note that the text of Numbers we have just referred to, as well as the last lines of Deuteronomy (Dt 34:10–12), aims at stressing the unique importance of Moses among all the prophets of Israel because of his exceptional familiarity with God. But in Ex 33:11 the same statement is made in an absolute way, in other words, without comparing him with the rest of the prophets. We can understand easily why soon enough in the Jewish-Hellenistic tradition of Philo of Alexandria and shortly thereafter in Christian tradition, Moses became the prototype of the person who prays.[1]

The first Christian writers began repeating this definition of prayer as conversation with God. "Praying is talking with God," said Gregory of Nyssa,[2] and Evagrius,[3] Jerome[4] and Augustine[5] echoed them. This, we believe, is the first spontaneous answer, which any simple Christian would give when asked what prayer is. In the seventh century, St. John Climacus would sum up and deepen this tradition: "Prayer in its very essence is a dialogue and union between a human being and God. In effect, it unites the world. It achieves reconciliation with God."[6] Here we find a new element. Prayer is a dialogue *and union.* Thus we see the emergence of the mystical tendency that has continued to develop in Christian prayer. Prayer is not just communicating with the divine Other, but becoming gradually united to this infinite Being. But note also the *cosmic* sense of that union: the whole universe is united in prayer. For the Greek, the human being is a microcosm, a little world rolled up in one. And in the Bible, the human being represents the whole of creation before God. Through us, the world prays.

But is prayer really a conversation with God? Anyone who reflects on this way of understanding prayer is bound to run into certain difficulties, because every conversation presupposes an exchange of ideas, experiences or affections between at least two interlocutors. And no one but the most hardened visionaries would claim that God intervenes in their prayer just as any other speaker does. This is true not only because we can't oblige God to answer us, but also because God is simply not on the same level as we are. If we were to use the language of everyday experience, we'd say that our prayer is more like a monologue. We say and believe that God listens to us, but we do not ordinarily have any experience of this. We know it by faith, and sometimes we experience it indirectly, when we interpret certain events as signs that God has heard us.

Referring to common experience, we say that *ordinarily* our prayer seems more like a monologue. In doing so, we have left open the possibility that on occasions God answers us. Sometimes theological reflection can be much more stringent than this. Karl Rahner, who described prayer as addressing ourselves to God throughout our life without obtaining any answer but the one we will receive after death, spoke ironically of the "pat and ready" solution offered by pious authors who interpret the inner movements and lights we sometimes receive in prayer as God answering us.[7] To be sure, psychology has made us somewhat more critical today than we used to be in the past. It is not hard for us to see how our own psyche can intervene in the answers we "hear." Today we are aware of how strongly our subconscious can suddenly surge up within us. Besides, we know that God does not communicate the way we do, in multiple words and limited concepts, one after another. These words we "hear" are at least to some extent our own words.

Even our "talking" with God needs to be rightly understood. We surely can't pretend to be informing, reminding or calling God's attention to something, since God, who is utterly actual consciousness, knows and is intimately present to all beings, closer to them than they are to themselves. Nor can we seriously imagine that when we ask God for anything for ourselves or others, we are moving God, or, so to speak, giving God one more motive for acting in a particular way. God loves us infinitely and doesn't need to be impelled by us to do something on our behalf. We talk to God in order to live our life, with all its sorrows and joys, in faith and love. Prayer consists in this: in drawing our person and our life, with all the affections and relationships that form part of them, into our relationship with the infinite God. This is where prayer as conversation finds its deepest meaning.

But the fact remains that to have a conversation properly so called, there has to be some sort of interchange. Prayer as speech is based on a faith in a transpersonal God. God is personal, eminently. That is to say, God is personal because God is infinite consciousness and love, who is immersed in the other, as Creator. But God is personal, eminently, or in a higher unique way, because God is not just one more limited individual among others. Jews, Christians and Moslems believe that God is revealed in our history, thus immersing the divine Self in our concrete existential situation. This grace of revelation is contained in the scriptures through which God continues to address us, initiating a dialogue. Even in this sense, prayer begins in God and our prayer is always a response to the grace of revelation. The fathers of the church have often repeated and commented on a recommendation made by St. Cyprian, bishop of Carthage in the third century: "Be constantly committed to prayer or to reading (the scriptures); by praying you speak to God, in reading God speaks to you."[8] But it seems to have been Augustine, a century later, who was more distinctively aware of the fact that prayer is always a response to revelation. He echoes Cyprian: "When you read, God speaks to you; when you pray, you speak to God."[9] Speaking very lovingly about his mother Monica, Augustine remembers: "she went twice a day, morning and evening without fail. . . to Thy church . . . to listen to Thy words and so that Thou wouldst hear her in her prayers."[10] The old monastic custom of having a short silent prayer after recitation of the psalms was intended to facilitate a personal answer to the divine words.

Yet the problem still subsists, at least to a certain extent. Did God become silent when the last book of the scriptures was finished or does God continue to address us? Is God not the Spirit who communicates with our spirit? Certainly revelation as an event is achieved in Jesus Christ and this revelation is contained and proclaimed in the scriptures. But the Spirit of God continues to address and move us. It is in this sense of an interpersonal relationship with God that the problem surfaces again. We must try to understand in which way God speaks to us. If a person is a consciousness and love which immerses itself in the other, and an interpersonal dialogue is the actualization of this relationship, we must remember that God is immersed in the other not as creatures are, partially and from the surface, but as their Creator, giving them being. Prayer is true conversation, but in a unique way, that is, not because God answers our words in a human way, with words. Karl Rahner put it very well when he said that we ourselves are the word uttered by God.[11] God speaks to us by creating us. Here, in this truth that our prayer begins in the act whereby God creates us and immerses the divine Self in us, do we find the answer to the dilemma that preoccupies some people so much in our days: Are these words we hear and these experiences we have in prayer from ourselves, or are they from God? To a certain extent this is a false dilemma, because God does not act from the outside, but from the depths of all our activities, as Creator. And we know that God may choose to be, as Spirit who communicates with our spirit, behind certain words and certain motions. God, orienting us toward the transcendent mystery, may become particularly present in some of our experiences. In this way (the mysterious divine ways) God can help us to find the answer we are seeking and can address and challenge us.

In certain profound experiences, the certainty of being in the presence of God or being under God's influence is so great that those who have these experiences cannot doubt them, at least as long as they last, although they may be able to communicate this certainty to others. In other cases, the charism of discernment, or of sudden insight, helps us discover the presence of the Spirit behind certain words or deeds. Much more often, however, there is need of discernment as a process of faith, in order to be able to distinguish those words that arise in our psyche as a divine message, in the midst of the innumerable words that we ourselves shape.

The dialogue with the divinity, in which prayer consists, is much, much more than an interchange of words (ideas or feelings) between a human being and God. Evagrius, passing from prayer to prayer life, exactly as Teresa of Jesus will do, centuries later, in her famous definition, speaks of intercourse and familiarity:

> Prayer is a continual intercourse of the spirit with God. What state of the soul then is required that the spirit might thus strain after its Master without wavering, living constantly with him without intermediary?[12]

Yes, prayer becomes living with God. And the communication flows at a deep level where words disappear. We must notice that in Teresa's classical description of the stages of prayer, there is an increasing reduction of words and activities. Prayer is a growing silence, a very communicative silence. A Syrian mystic (c. 600 A.D.), Abraham of Nathpar, wrote these beautiful sentences:

> There is a silence of the tongue, there is a silence of the whole body, there is the silence of the soul, there is the

silence of the mind, and there is the silence of the spirit. . . . The silence of the spirit is when the mind ceases even from stirrings caused by spiritual beings, and when all its movements are stirred solely by Being; in this state it is truly silent, aware that the silence which is upon it is itself silent.[13]

Prayer as a Lifting Up

Christian tradition has also given us another definition that I believe is more profound, or at least less problematical: Prayer is the lifting up of our hearts and minds to God. Origen stated this in the third century, in a comment on verse 1 of the 25th Psalm: "To thee, O Lord, I lift up my soul."

What David says is, "To you have I lifted up my eyes, you who dwell in heaven" (Ps 123:1) and "To you, O God, have I lifted up my soul" (Ps 25:1). For the eyes of the mind are lifted up from their preoccupation with earthly things and from their being filled with the impression of material things. And they are so exalted that they peer beyond the created order and arrive at the sheer contemplation of God and at conversing with Him reverently and suitably as He listens. How would things so great fail to profit these eyes that gaze at the glory of the Lord with unveiled face and that are being changed into His likeness from glory to glory (cf. 2 Cor 3:18)? For then they partake of some divine and intelligible radiance. And the soul is lifted up and following the Spirit is separated from the body. Not only does it follow the Spirit, it then comes to be in Him.[14]

Origen's comment is very suggestive. He begins with a certain neoplatonic accent (prayer is a lifting up from the earthly to the heavenly) and ends with the first Christian description (no longer neoplatonic!) of ecstasis, when the soul is lifted up by the Spirit, in a sense, out of its body. The neoplatonic accent is echoed and reinforced in a sermon attributed to St. Augustine.[15] In the ancient Eastern Church, prayer as a lifting up to God was dealt with, among others, by Evagrius of Pontus[16] and John Damascene.[17] Remember, too, that even now the presider at the eucharist, at the beginning of the great central prayer, invites those present to lift up their hearts to God, that is, to accompany him in prayer.

It is clear that by heart or mind one does not mean simply the inwardness of the person. Those who pray lift themselves up entirely to God, with their life, their work, their relationships and their affections. They do so with their consciousness and their love, of course, but they lift up their all, or at least they try to do so. It's not just a matter of lifting up their thought through reflection.

We are clearly using a spatial image here, an image of height, which is quite adequate, because it is a symbolic representation of the divine transcendence, of God's being above all things. Not because God dwells only or especially in some higher part of the universe. Any star is just as close to its Creator as the earth is. With equal truth we can use the image of depth, referring to the divine immanence, that is to say, God's presence in the inmost of our being. Augustine found God in the depth of himself, after having looked for God outside and discovered that God was deeper within him "than his innermost depths."[18] God is in the very source and root of our being, as Creator. Praying, in this sense, is drawing back our persons, our lives, our labors, our joys and sufferings, our relationships, to that depth in which we are created by God. It is something like running the tape of creation backward to its beginning. We are not talking about a simple subjective interiorization, a simple encounter with ourselves (mere reflection is not prayer), but about a radical interiorization to the point of finding ourselves, beyond ourselves, in the infinite being who creates us.

At the Very Core: Presence and Relation

In reality, the two definitions of prayer, namely, as conversation with God or as an encounter with the divinity in the heights or in the depths, point in the same direction: toward an interpretation of prayer as presence and as relation.

Prayer, in Christianity as well as in Judaism, in Islam or in certain forms of Hinduism, essentially consists in opening oneself up in the presence of that infinite being who is present to us as Creator. Christianity has, moreover, kept insisting on the presence of God in us through grace, lifting us up toward the divinity and making us sharers in the divine nature. The gratuitous love of God thus becomes an objective reality in us. Prayer, then, is an opening up of ourselves to this presence that creates and transforms us. Recall that for St. Paul, the Spirit (God in transcendent singularity) dwells in our hearts (Rom 5:5, 8:9). Praying certainly does not mean making God present in us or in our lives. God is already there. It means becoming aware of this presence and making ourselves present to God in faith, hope and charity.

In the twelfth century, William of St. Thierry summed up his whole teaching on prayer in this recommendation he gave for the formation of beginners: "Beginners would be taught to draw near to God so that God in turn may draw near to them."[19] Translating this into more precise language, we might say that those who pray draw near to God so that the Spirit may reveal God's nearness to them. *Drawing near to God:* all prayer consists in this. The successive degrees of prayer will consist precisely of an intensification of the awareness of the divine presence, of an ever increasing drawing near to God and of a growing awareness of God's active loving presence. Praying is our being present to the One who is present to us in love.

But at the same time, all of this implies that praying

means establishing an interpersonal relationship with God. We do not discover a thing, but a personal being. We have already said that God is personal in an eminent degree, that is, without the limitations of the notion human personhood implies: a being, pure consciousness and infinite liberty, who immerses the divine self in others, by creating them and lifting them up to that self. We can see, then, why Teresa of Jesus defined prayer as an "intimate sharing between friends."[20] Long before Teresa, Evagrius of Pontus, one of the most prestigious masters of primitive monasticism, had defined prayer as "a continual intercourse of the spirit with God."[21]

It is a well-known fact that for the Jewish philosopher Martin Buber the I/Thou relationship between the human being and God constitutes the fundamental structure of biblical religious expression. This is a deep truth, although it needs to be somewhat nuanced. The divine Thou whom the human I addresses is not just one limited individual among others who appear in one's life. God is the infinite Thou who embraces all things and in whom all things come into being and find their ultimate meaning. Moreover, the human thou whom God addresses is not a subject who exists in grand independence, but is, rather, one of God's creatures, a being who has his or her whole reason for being in God. God creates the terminus of the divine-human dialogue of relationship. God speaks and relates by creating.

Here, we believe, is the essence of prayer: in being present and in being related. In essence, prayer is not an activity, that is, a speaking, but rather a mode of being which is actualized and expressed in that activity. Praying is being open to the presence who creates us, being aware of the unique relationship which unites us to God. Praying is being and living a faith-commitment to the God who reveals (gives) the divine self to us. Prayers, being radically a way of being before God, can be more readily grasped on the model of human love. A human lover is not so much one who does something, as one who lives open to a loved being, although this relationship may well be expressed in words, gestures and actions, and nourished by them.

From what we have said, we can better understand something that the witnesses of the Spirit tell us about prayer. The third gospel attributes this teaching to Christ himself: "He told them a parable on the necessity of praying always and not losing heart" (Lk 18:1). St. Paul repeats this notion frequently: "Rejoice always, never cease praying, render constant thanks; such is God's will for you in Christ Jesus" (1 Thes 5:16–17). "Be filled with the Spirit. . . . Give thanks to God the Father always and for everything . . . " (Eph 5:18–20). The primitive monks and nuns understood prayer without ceasing as the sum and substance of their vocation.[22] Monks, we are told, "talk constantly with God." Evagrius used to counsel them, "Pray without interruption."[23] Hence their vocation in the church came to be called the "angelic life" because, like the angels, they were always in God's presence. Centuries later, St. Bernard gave the same advice.[24] And one of St. Francis of Assisi's first biographers wrote: "It was not just a matter of his praying much, but rather of his becoming a prayer."[25] Neither Luke, nor Paul, nor the hermits of the desert, nor St. Bernard were exaggerating, because none of them was thinking of prayer as an activity, but rather as a constant orientation which often becomes conscious. Augustine explained several times that it is in our constant desire of God that we pray without cease: "That true Life taught us to pray . . . and not to pray with much speaking. . . . Yet He said: 'we ought always to pray and not to faint' . . . We pray always, with insistent desire in that same faith, hope and charity."[26]

The Christian mystics, St. Teresa of Jesus in particular, have described the ultimate degree of the spiritual life— the transforming union—as being characterized by an habitual sense of the presence of God. God remains continually, like a light, in the experience of the mystic who, with very great frequency, directs his or her attention to God. Whoever has been tenderly or passionately in love has some notion of what this means.

Anyone who thinks of prayer mainly or solely as an activity like thinking or speaking is woefully wrong. This is the case with those who dedicate themselves to "saying prayers" without regard for living lovingly in God's presence. For them, prayer becomes a human work, a product of our own which makes us feel satisfied and justified. May God forgive us and make us see our blindness. But equally in error are those who, because they are so terribly busy, abandon prayer altogether or reduce it to something more or less sporadic, because they believe it's a matter of activities for which they don't have the time or energy. People like this will have to think about living in God's presence, feeling their being in God and for God. Prayer as an activity will then become easier for them, or at least more strengthening, even though they may not be able to devote as much time to it as others do.

Prayer and Intimacy

Every human being feels a twofold need. In the first place, there is the need to be known as this particular person and not just as one more face among countless other faces. We normally expect this recognition from those who are nearest to us. In the second place, there is the need to be able to reveal our own feelings to certain others. More or less consciously, by an instinctively felt affinity or by a decision based on experience, we tend to arrange others in concentric circles around us according to the degree of intensity with which we relate to them. The greater or lesser degree of relationship we feel for them, the greater or lesser amount of information we give them concerning our inner feelings. Husband or wife is mainly in the center, then parents and children, sweethearts, intimates, friends, fellow workers and acquaintances: the circles usually broaden and communications usually lessen as we move outward in this order.

In our days this need for intimacy seems to have grown even more acute. Significantly, it is largely in the United States, with its great urban masses, that intimacy is spoken of most insistently. It is a constant topic in books on spirituality and psychology, in spiritual direction, in therapy sessions and in counseling. People talk about physical intimacy or lack of it (for example, in celibacy), about psychological intimacy and about intimate spiritual relationships. The marked tendency toward communion and participation in contemporary spirituality is countered in North America with the sense of isolation and anonymity felt by those of us who live in great cities. Prayer groups allow us to meet together person-to-person and at the same time to express, at least partially, our need for spiritual intimacy.

The believer, in personal prayer, puts God in the very center of the concentric circles that spread outward from greater intimacy (the smaller circles) toward lesser intimacy (the broader circles). We have already remarked that prayer is not just interiorization, but rather an entering into ourselves to the depths where we find ourselves in God and transcend ourselves. We find ourselves as persons in this sense with a personal God, at a depth in which we do not find ourselves with any human person. Before God we are always this unique man or this unique woman, because it is God who creates us in our singularity. And we confess to God what we would not reveal even to husband or wife, father or mother, or intimate friend. The only things we don't confess to God are the things that we dare not confess even to ourselves. But in prayer, sustained by faith and enveloped in an atmosphere of love, we finally come to confess even those things we have heretofore dreaded to acknowledge about ourselves. Authentic prayer is hence the most radically personalizing act. In it we recognize ourselves and know that we are recognized in our authentic personality, with all its positive and negative sides, its strengths and weaknesses.

The way of prayer is characterized by growing intimacy, because this way is at once a progressive entering into ourselves and an ever more total commitment of ourselves to God. The fact that when we face ourselves in the depths of ourselves we do not meet an individual, but rather the infinite and transcendent mystery of divinity, confers on this intimacy an utterly particular quality. Since it is not individual, it does not suffer from the limits that are imposed by our own limitations. It allows total self-commitment. But at the same time, since God is infinite, our relationship with the divinity in prayer always has something of the mysterious and unattainable about it. There is no self-gift like God's self-gift to us, since God's self-gift is made through creation. Yet at the same time God eludes us. The divine mystery is always beyond our concepts and our images. This leads to a continual transcending of our thoughts about God and a periodic death for our symbols of divinity. Prayer is always an encounter in faith. This leads us, as no other relation does, to go out of ourselves.

We have been talking about intimacy with God, not of closing ourselves up in our own intimacy. Prayer entails the twofold movement of entering into ourself, becoming aware of our own situation, and of going out of ourself in order to share this intimate experience with God. Prayer is getting out of ourself, breaking through our own solitude, throwing open our inmost windows and crying out for help. Praying is living in company, even when, on the level of sensibility, this friendly presence may not be felt.

Prayer, a Divine Gift

Thus far in our reflections on prayer we have been focusing on the human side of prayer—what we ourselves do—although we have been able to glimpse between the lines what God does.

Nevertheless, prayer begins in God. In the first place, God becomes present to us and begins the relationship by creating us and by revealing the divine being to us. Every prayer, then, is a response. First, God speaks to us in the twofold sense that God utters us by creating us and reveals the divine being to us in our history. Praying is accepting this divine initiative and developing it on our part.

But there's more to it than that. In the second place, it is a grace of God that someone becomes aware of God's presence and responds to it. Augustine of Hippo stated this quite clearly: "That we pray at all is a gift of God."[27] Evagrius of Pontus likewise stressed it: "If you wish to pray it is God whom you need. God is the One who gives prayer to the person who prays."[28]

To explain this, Origen[29] and St. Augustine[30] and, centuries after him, Luther,[31] had recourse to St. Paul's teaching on the relations that exist between the Spirit and prayer. For St. Paul, prayer is the act proper of the Spirit, that is, the divine Spirit becomes present in our lives above all by praying. And every Christian prayer is the fruit of this action:

> All who are led by the Spirit of God are sons and daughters of God. You did not receive a spirit of slavery leading you back into fear, but a spirit of adoption through which we cry out, "Abba!" (that is, "Father"). The Spirit gives witness with our spirit that we are children of God (Rom 8:14–16).

> The proof that you are sons and daughters of God is the fact that God has sent forth into our hearts the spirit of his Son which cries out "Abba!" ("Father!") (Gal 4:6).

In the scriptures of Israel, the Spirit of God already appears above all in two contexts. On the one hand, the Spirit appears as the mysterious and transcendent God who enters into our lives and touches us, by making us prophesy or by giving us a superhuman power or wisdom. On the other hand, the Spirit appears precisely as God, giver of life. Both of these aspects seem to be fused in the Christian scriptures, especially in St. Paul. The Spirit, in mysterious uniqueness, descends upon us and lifts us up to God by means of faith, making us God's sons and daughters. This communion makes possible the filial relationship referred to in the two texts we cited (Rom 8:14–16; Gal 4:6). Note that a few verses later in the letter to the Romans, Paul adds something very important:

> The Spirit too helps us in our weakness, for we do not know how to pray as we ought; but the Spirit makes intercession for us with groanings that cannot be expressed in speech. God who searches hearts knows what the Spirit means, for the Spirit intercedes for the saints as God wills (Rom 8:26–27).

Here the Spirit is the one who prays in us. Our prayer is an activity of the Spirit of God. St. Paul repeats the same idea in the text of the letter to the Galatians.

Now we understand what Evagrius meant when he said that if we wish to pray we only need God. We have to do two things, then: to ask God for the gift of prayer and to open ourselves docilely to the action of his Spirit. The important thing is not what we are going to do (we ourselves pray in the Spirit and with the Spirit), but rather what the divine Spirit is going to do. The Spirit communicates with God, with herself, at a depth that is beyond our concepts. St. Paul speaks of this prayer as "groanings" that cannot be humanly translated.

We noted above that prayer has been described as lifting ourselves up to God. Now we have to interpret it in a new key: Prayer is being lifted up by the Spirit to God.

Perhaps we should go deeper still: Praying, according to what we have been discovering in Christian tradition and above all in St. Paul, is actuating our filial communion with God. In prayer, we find ourselves between the Spirit of God who communicates the gift of filiation to us, and the mystery of the divinity itself in its very source, the Father. In prayer we find ourselves within the mystery of the Trinity: in the presence of God the source of everything, with the Son, lifted up and moved by the maternal Spirit of God. Almost in our own days, a young French Carmelite nun, Sister Elizabeth of the Trinity, has reminded us of this by developing her spiritual life as a communion with the Blessed Trinity.

Accepting the Gift: Fidelity

If prayer is, radically, grace, then the believer must open himself or herself to it with fidelity and perseverance. The only thing that God asks of us is that we persevere in humble faith. The need for persevering prayer is stressed in all Christian churches. The example of Jesus (which we will consider later) and that of the primitive church (Acts 1:14; 2:42; 6:4) and the frequent recommendations of the apostle Paul (1 Thes 1:2–3; 2:13; 3:10; 5:17; 1 Cor 1:4; Rom 1:9–10; 12:12; cf. Lk 18:1) are decisive for everyone. Luther, in one of those pithy and folksy sayings he was so fond of, stated that "the Christian should pray, just as the shoemaker makes shoes and the tailor makes clothes."[32]

The insistence of Jesus and of the scriptures on this matter invites us to reflect on the question, "Why is prayer so necessary for us?" It is so necessary because through prayer we accept God's grace and submit ourselves to it. This does not mean that by praying we are going to effect our own salvation or sanctification. Only God saves and sanctifies. But through prayer we open ourselves up to this grace and let it penetrate our consciousness and our will. It would not be out of place for us to insist on the fact that prayer is nothing else than an expression of faith, hope and charity.

But wouldn't our participation in the church's worship be enough? To be sure, this is fundamental, because the liturgy, besides being the prayer of the Christian community, is also the action of Christ. But liturgical action should be carried over into the rest of our life through personal prayer. On the one hand, from the second century on, Christian tradition (as we will presently see) has been recommending that we strive to digest and assimilate the strong food that God gives us in the word and the eucharist. Personal prayer is always a continuation of the liturgy, a meditation on the word we have heard and a savoring of the grace we have received. On the other hand, those who have lived the liturgy intensely always feel touched by love and need to go on expressing this love. At a certain point in the spiritual journey, prayer begins to be perceived as a need, and one feels the lack of it. St. Augustine speaks frequently of desire as the source of prayer—a desire for the blessed life, a desire for God.[33] It is this continual desire (this "hunger" for God) that tends to make prayer continual, even when one is not always praying. Julian of Norwich also says that prayer is born of a yearning for God.[34] And John of the Cross described the way of prayer as a going out in search of the Beloved. Seeking God, the face of God, is one of the commonest expressions in the piety of Israel.

There comes a moment, the moment when the love of God fully catches fire in us, and prayer becomes something spontaneous, like breathing. This was the ideal of primitive and medieval monasticism. In a few words we have quoted before, Luther compares this spontaneous constant prayer to the pulse, always beating, even when we are sleeping. This is the same ideal that John Wesley repeatedly proposed to Christians in his *Plain Account:* "we pray," he wrote, "because we love, and we love, because he first loved us."[35] Exactly.

How St. Teresa of Jesus Understood Prayer

The great sixteenth century Carmelite, commonly acknowledged to be the teacher par excellence in matters of prayer long before Paul VI declared her a doctor of the church, reflects in numerous texts what she thought to be the very essence of prayer. But she does so above all in a passage from her autobiography. Perhaps because it was the first book she wrote (it was finished in June 1562, six months before she began her *Way of Perfection*), she wanted to express precisely what she meant by prayer. We are going to take this definition—which is most popular among spiritual writers and preachers—as a basic text, citing in connection with its various elements other less complete definitions she gave on other occasions.

The essential elements of the two traditional definitions of prayer which we have been considering are, we believe, contained in Teresa's definition. She is speaking in the context of mental prayer, but it must be remembered that for her the difference between vocal, pronounced prayer, and mental, purely interior prayer, is rather inadequate, since she holds that even vocal prayer must proceed from the mind and is thus somehow mental. Precisely for those who were for some reason afraid to embark on the ways of mental prayer, Madre Teresa recommended that while they were reciting the Our Father they should fix their attention on God and enter into communion with the Son of God who taught us that prayer.[36] It would be well for us now to reflect on the definition of prayer she has given us, because it sets the essentials of Christian prayer in high relief, explicitly stating, better than the two traditional definitions, some of its characteristics.

> Mental prayer in my opinion is nothing else than an intimate sharing between friends; it means taking time frequently to be alone with Him who we know loves us.[37]

Leaving aside the words "taking time frequently to be alone"—which refer to the life of prayer as a frequent actualization in solitude, at least that of the heart, of our encounter with God—we are left with the Castilian mystic's fundamental notion of prayer: Prayer is an intimate, friendly sharing (*tratar de amistad*) with one who we know loves us. In the saint's language, *tratar* or *trato* has a special nuance of meaning. It refers, of course, to a communication, but it goes deeper than that, connoting an interpersonal relationship. Hence it goes beyond the idea of "conversation with God," and is based on the encounter itself between persons. Teresa explicitly states a new element: friendship between God and the human being. Prayer is a relationship of friendship.

Here, Teresa reflects something of her own pronounced penchant for friendship. Her letters are filled with expressions of affection for her great men and women friends: St. Peter of Alcántra, Fr. Baltasar Alvarez, Fr. Jerónimo Gracián, Fr. Domingo Báñez, Doña Guiomar de Ulloa and some of her own nuns. In fact, this penchant for friendship with spiritual persons seems to have hindered her committing herself definitively to God in *trato de amistad*, until the occasion when she beheld "the most extraordinary beauty of Christ"[38] and gave herself to him without reserve. But it should be remarked that Teresa is echoing here what the Bible itself reveals on friendship with God. The tender spousal love of God for Israel that appears in Hosea (Hos 2:16–22), the promise of Jesus in Luke: "In my kingdom you will eat and drink at my table" (Lk 22:30), or in John: "I no longer speak to you as slaves. . . . Instead, I call you friends" (Jn 15:15), or in the book of Revelation: "If anyone hears me calling and opens the door, I will enter . . . and have supper with him, and he with me" (Rev 3:20)—all of these texts must have caught Madre Teresa's attention.

Teresa of Jesus understood friendship as an interchange of affections[39] which is expressed in and nourished by gifts and communications, and which leads to intimacy.[40] It would not be out of place to recall that for St. Thomas Aquinas, "Charity is a form of friendship,"[41] understanding friendship to mean a generous love that desires and seeks the good of the other.

That Teresa viewed prayer as being above all a relation of friendship is confirmed from other texts by her. She speaks of the beginnings of prayer as a "wish to have friendship with God," a "wish to love and please God,"[42] and of contemplation as "close friendship."[43] She was aware, nevertheless, that this friendship with God, expressed and nourished in prayer, could take on the color and savor of the various love-relationships which human beings experience. She counseled her nuns: "Speak with Him as with a father, or a brother, or a lord, or as with a spouse; sometimes in one way, at other times in another; He will teach you what you must do in order to please Him."[44] A few lines earlier, she had spoken of God as "a Guest." God's reality sums up and surpasses all these varied experiences of love.

After defining prayer as a friendly relationship, Teresa says something that is not explicitly contained in the two traditional definitions, although we have discovered it throughout Christian tradition, starting from St. Paul. This relationship and communication of love has its point of departure in the knowledge that God loves us: "Prayer is an intimate sharing between friends . . . with the One who we know loves us." Prayer is, then, a response, a corresponding in love with the one who began loving us. In Teresa, too, prayer begins in God. She says as much in another passage: "I'm not asking you to do anything more than look at Him . . . your Spouse never takes his eyes off you."[45] Prayer as contemplation is thus setting ourselves to look on the one who is constantly looking on us with love. In the *Way of Perfection*, speaking of the life of prayer, she writes: "Behold it is a beautiful exchange to give our love for His."[46]

We know full well that it is God's love for us that creates our love for God and for our neighbor. To love God is always to respond to God with the same love which God gives us.

This "knowing" that God loves us can be understood in two ways. In the first place, we know it by faith. Faith is accepting the revelation of a God who loves us and then entrusting ourselves to God. This is the essential and never-failing knowledge we must have. Praying is always a response of faith to God's grace and must always be founded on faith. It does not consist in feeling, but rather in believing. But there comes a moment when faith becomes deeply rooted in us through the gifts of the Spirit (above all the gift of wisdom which gives us a relish for the things of God), and produces in us an experience of God's love. In prayer, one begins by simply believing in the love of God and one ends by believing and savoring: we feel loved by God. It is then that love invades us fully. The experience of being loved by God produces in us living flames of love for God and for our neighbor in God. To each of the two different ways or levels of "knowing" there is a correspondingly different way of prayer as a response.

It is quite clear that, for Teresa of Jesus, prayer is above all love. She has clearly written as much in *The Book of Foundations:*

> For I have run into some for whom it seems the whole business (or prayer) lies in thinking. . . . I do not deny that it is a favor from the Lord if someone is able to be always meditating on His works, and it is good that one strive to do so. However, it must be understood that not all imaginations are by their nature capable of this meditating, but all souls are capable of loving. . . . Hence, the soul's progress does not lie in thinking much but in loving much.[47]

She expresses the same thought in *The Interior Castle:*

> In order to profit from this path and ascend to the dwelling places we desire, the important thing is not

to think much but to love much; and so, do that which best stirs you to love.[48]

But she also says quite clearly what this love consists in: "It doesn't consist in great delight but in desiring with strong determination to please God in everything."[49] It is not, then, a matter of sentimentalism, but of committing oneself totally to God.

2

Jesus and Prayer

The men and women who followed Jesus became his disciples when they encountered the grace of God in Jesus, in his words and actions, in the healings he performed, in his dealings with sinners and outcasts and, in a new way, after the scandal of the cross, in his resurrection. We too are Christians because we encounter God in Christ Jesus, who died and is risen for us; we do so through faith, baptism and the eucharist, and because, together with the community of his disciples, we are trying to assimilate his Spirit by recalling his words and his actions. It is necessary for us to return to Jesus in order to confront our ideas on prayer with the teachings of Jesus, and to compare our experience of prayer with what the gospels tell us concerning the prayer of the Son of God.[1]

Jesus Prays

We can't allow ourselves to harbor the illusion that the gospels contain a "life of Jesus" in the sense in which the terms *life* and *biography* have come to be understood since the time of the nineteenth century positivist thinkers. The gospels were written in order to proclaim, announce and teach. But the gospels proclaim the grace of God that has been given us definitively in Jesus, precisely by *narrating* the original Christian experience, meaning not only the experience which the apostles had of Jesus, but also, through their experience, the experience of Jesus himself, his relationship with the Father, and with the men and women who surrounded him. Through various kinds of stories and of sayings remembered or attributed to Jesus, the gospels give us a portrait of Jesus, recalling to us his faith in the reign of God, his ministry, his struggles, etc.

We are concerned here with the theme of prayer in Jesus. The gospels frequently present Jesus in prayer. Luke notably multiplies incidents portraying Jesus at prayer which are not mentioned in the other evangelists (Lk 3:21, cf. Mk 1:10 and Mt 3:12; Lk 6:12, cf. Mk 3:13 and Mt 10:1; Lk 11:1, cf. Mt 6:9; Lk 9:18, 28–29, cf. Mk 9:2 and Mt 17:1–2). In one instance, a general statement of Luke ("He often retired to deserted places and prayed," Lk 5:16) seems to have been inspired by one of the three texts in which Mark speaks of Jesus' prayer: Mk 1:35 ("Rising early the next morning, he went off to a lonely place in the desert; there he was absorbed in prayer"). All of this seems to reflect the particular importance that prayer held for Luke. But this was possible only because the most ancient traditions collected in the gospels insist on presenting Jesus to us in prayer.

"Jesus was a Jew who prayed like a Jew."[2] He prayed before and after meals (Mt 14:19, 15:36, 16:26–27); he took part in the sabbath service (Mt 9:35; Mk 1:21–39; 3:1; 6:2, Lk 4:16–28); he periodically visited the temple, which he seems to have considered "a house of prayer" (Mk 11:17). All of these things characterized him as a pious Jew.

But there was also something distinctive to Jesus, something that characterized him and no one else: his personal, spontaneous prayer. With some frequency we see him withdraw to a mountain, a solitary place or a garden to pray (Mk 1:35; 6:46; 14:32). We already noted how Luke felt no hesitation at generalizing this. He even tells us that on one occasion Jesus "went out to the mountain to pray, spending the night in communion with God" (Lk 6:12). Although this is one of the texts in which Luke alone speaks of the prayer of Jesus, there seems to have been a historical remembrance behind it. We glimpse something of it in Mk 1:35, where Jesus, after a long and exhausting day of ministry, spent part of the night in prayer. The story of Gethsemani confirms it.

Jesus' prayer was in fact so spontaneous that the gospels tell us that he occasionally addressed his Father publicly, before the crowd (Mt 11:42; cf. Jn 11:41–42; 12:28; 17:1–26).

This commitment of Jesus to prayer is very significant, because, if we read the gospels attentively, we can observe in him a continuous atmosphere of prayer in the midst of an intense ministry. Jesus discovers the loving presence of his Abba not only in the lilies of the field and the birds of the air (Mt 6:26–30), but also, and perhaps above all, in human beings who are suffering. They brought a paralytic to him, lowering the poor man down through a hole they made in the roof, and Jesus' first reaction is "Son, God has forgiven you your sins" (Mk 2:1–6—the use of the passive is a pious way to avoid saying the holy name of the Lord). He would later say the same to a woman who broke into the banquet given by a Pharisee (Lk 7:48). Jesus sees the compassion-filled face of his Abba looking on the sinner, and he proclaims the divine pardon. Jesus thus shows himself to be a great contemplative. He contemplates his Father and does what he sees his Father doing (Jn 5:19); he hears his Father and proclaims what he has heard (Jn 8:28).

And nevertheless, despite his living in the Father's presence, loving and serving him in the ministry he entrusted to him, Jesus still feels the need to withdraw in order to spend some hours alone, immersed in the fountainhead of his being. The Markan text we cited above is really surprising. Very early in the morning, well before dawn, Jesus slips quietly from the house and goes outside town to pray in solitude (Mk 1:35). Projecting our own experiences on him, we cannot doubt that Jesus felt the need to withdraw in order to immerse himself expressly in the presence and thus in faith to revive his life, his joys, his conflicts and his relationships. He had a need of solitude as a privileged place to rest in love, as an ideal situation in which to discern the mysterious ways of his Abba and to confront his life and ministry with the will of the one who sent him. Prayer, a conscious and reflective encounter of his humanity with the divine mystery, both nourished and strengthened him.

Filial Relationship

Typical of Jesus is his way of addressing God, calling him *Abba*, daddy.[3] *Abba* originally belonged to the language of childhood. This is what little children called their fathers. But in Jesus' time, *abba* was commonly used by adults as a respectful and affectionate term of address to their father. In the Greek text of Mk 14:36 (the prayer in Gethsemani), it is cited in Aramaic. St. Paul does the same twice, echoing an earlier tradition: "A Spirit . . . through which we cry out, 'Abba!' " (Rom 8:15), and "The Spirit of his Son which cries out 'Abba!' " (Gal 4:6). But the exegetes believe that the Greek term *Pater*, "Father" in Mt 11:25–26, is a translation of the original *Abba* in Aramaic. They hold this also with respect to the initial *Pater* of the Lord's Prayer in Luke's more primitive form (Lk 11:2), which Matthew's church had translated in a way more conformable to Jewish reverential sensibilities as *our* Father *who art in heaven* (Mt 6:9). Those who pray the Lord's Prayer in Matthew's version are so to speak hidden in the group ("our") and God appears at once as Father and sovereign ("in heaven"). The intimate, individual relationship which Jesus expressed in his *Abba* was somewhat shocking to ordinary Jewish sensibilities.

It is clear enough that Jesus lived out his relationship with the God from whom he proceeded (as Son, prophet, word and image) as an intimate relationship of mingled trust, love and respect. He projected on this relationship the experience he had had in his infancy with Joseph. In the patriarchal family the father was everything: the source of sustenance, the authority, the first and often the only educator of his sons. Recall that on one occasion, according to a tradition common to Matthew and Luke, Jesus attributed a kind of paternal love to God in order to arouse his listeners' trust in prayer: "What father among you, if his son asks for a fish, will give him a serpent instead. . . . How much more will your Father in heaven . . . " (cf. Lk 11:11–13; Mt 7:9–11). "In praying do not heap up empty phrases . . . for your Father knows what you need before you ask him" (Mt 6:7–8).

Today, when the situation of man and woman in the family is so different from what it was in Jesus' day, this name *abba*, which was meant to convey only confidence, love and respect, is somewhat obscured for us by the masculine accent of the symbol, because the role then played by the father is now shared equally by fathers and mothers, and our mother is often the one who provides the bread and better understands our needs. But it should be noted that the masculine element is not what is central to the symbol, but is totally exterior to it. The symbol is meant to express provident love, tender care and protection. Hence today one might either leave it in its original Aramaic, to reflect the original usage of Jesus, or else translate it as papa or mama, father or mother.

In fact, Jesus himself seems to have projected on God not only the face of Joseph, but also the maternal cares of Mary. In the Mediterranean family (whether Jewish, Greek or Roman), it was mainly the mother who cared for the birds, and only she who tended the flowers and plants. (This is still the case today. I never once saw my own father feed our canaries, let alone water the plants. My mother is still doing it patiently and lovingly to this day.) And yet Jesus speaks of the love with which God feeds the birds and clothes the lilies of the field.

More by Example Than by Teaching

If we pay attention to what Jesus says about prayer, we will note that it is precious little and some of it is rather negative. Don't put yourselves narcissistically in the center of your prayer like that Pharisee who went up to the temple to tell God how content he was with himself; rather, prostrate yourself humbly before God's mercy, like that publican (Lk 18:10–14). Don't pray in order to be seen (Mt 6:5). Don't believe that by calling me Lord, Lord, you're going to enter the reign of heaven (Mt 7:21). Don't act in a pious way in order to defraud widows of their money (Mk 12:38). Don't make the temple, which is a house of prayer, into a market or a den of thieves (Mk 11:7; Mt 21:13; Lk 19:46; Jn 2:16).

Compared with these cautions on how we ought not to pray, Jesus' positive teachings on prayer seem to be even more reduced. Obviously he accepted the prayer of petition, contrariwise to the Greek and Roman philosophers, who considered it useless and even offensive (since we surely can't pretend to inform God of something God doesn't already know, nor can we try to change God's will). We may go even further than this and say that Jesus referred almost exclusively to the prayer of petition. In his eyes, human beings appear as creatures and sinners, dependent on God and in need of his grace. Jesus does, however, agree with the Stoics in stating that God has no need to be informed by us of our needs: Your *abba* in heaven (an image quite alien to philosophy) knows what you need before you ask (Mt 6:8; cf. 6:32). Then why ask at all? Because, as we shall see in a moment, when we ask for a remedy for some need, we must always ask God that God's will, not ours, be done. We're not attempting to change God's will or to give God some further reason for acting: God already loves us infinitely. What we want to do is enter into the saving will of God. But we do this by living in faith our weakness and need. We lift up to God, that is, we take stock, in faith, in the divine presence, of our needs, and we acknowledge above all that we have need of God.

Above all, Jesus recommends faith, that is, faith in God's power and trust in God's goodness. Nevertheless he told us that we should seek first the reign of God and that all the rest would be given us in addition (Mt 6:33; cf. Lk 12:31). To seek means not only to orient ourselves toward this reign, but to ask God to establish it. A saying attributed to Jesus by extrabiblical tradition (Clement, Origen, Eusebius and Ambrose) states: "Ask for the great and God will give you the little in addition."[4] The "great" is doubtless God's grace, God's reign. The gospel of Mark transmits yet another teaching of Jesus on prayer: We have to draw near to pray with a generous heart, forgiving the offenses of others against us, thus imitating the one who forgives us. Prayer must spring, then, from a life that is animated by love (cf. Mk 11:25–26).

One curious note in this respect is the fact that Jesus does not seem to have taught, prescribed or recommended any set prayers for his own group or for others. Together with his disciples, he doubtless said the customary prayers at synagogue services and before and after meals. But according to Luke, Jesus' own disciples noted that the Baptizer taught prayers to his disciples, while Jesus did not. According to this text, it was only at the request of the disciples that Jesus taught them the very brief prayer of the Our Father (Lk 11:1–4). It is clear, however, that he gave them the example of his own personal commitment to prayer in solitude. In fact, the same Lukan text tells us that it was precisely after seeing him in prayer that they asked him to teach them some prayer (Lk 11:1). It seems that Jesus set a very high value on personal prayer as an expression of one's own relationship with God. In contrast, even though he accepted the customary community prayers, he seems not to have attached too much importance to them, fearing perhaps that they might become fossilized rituals.

It is quite significant that John, who was distinguished for his fasting and whom Jesus himself characterized as a player of dirges (Lk 7:32–33), should have taught prayers to his disciples (Lk 11:1). If these gospel-data transmit a historical remembrance of John, it is clear that the latter's group was more ritualized, while Jesus' group was much freer in this respect. For Jesus, prayer had to break forth as a spontaneous expression of one's own intimate feelings, from one's own faith, hope and love.

Prayer and Faith

Let us now turn our attention to the intimate relationship that Jesus saw between faith and prayer. Jesus frequently exhorts us, when he is speaking of prayer, to have faith. Faith, for Jesus, is essentially trust in the absolute power of God and in God's merciful attitude toward us. Such was the faith of the centurion (Mt 8:5–13) and of the Syrophoenician woman (Mk 7:24–30); the faith Jesus referred to in speaking to the father of the epileptic boy (Mk 9:23) and which he apparently found lacking in his disciples (Mk 9:18–19); the faith that could dry up a fig tree and move mountains (Mk 11:21–22). Everything is possible to one who believes (Mk 9:22–23; 11:24). This doesn't mean that prayer has an automatic value. For it is not enough to say, Lord, Lord, to enter into God's reign. Prayer has to be the expression of a life attuned to the saving will of God (Mt 7:21). This is exactly what prayer means for Jesus: believing in the sovereign power and gratuitous love of God in such a way that our whole life is impregnated with this faith and open to the mysterious presence of God in all things, even the smallest ones. The God whom Jesus preaches is a sovereign God, mysterious yet at the same time very close to us in mercy. Whoever has God or is in God in this way is most powerful indeed.

Prayer and God's Will

That the prayer of petition does not serve to bring God around to our way of thinking, but rather unites us to what God wants, appears very clearly in Jesus. There is a prayer transmitted in the source common to Matthew (11:22–26) and Luke (10:21–22) which seems to be the very echo of a prayer of Jesus:

> Thank you, Abba, Lord of heaven and earth, for you have hidden these things from the wise and clever and have revealed them to mere children. Yes, Abba, you have graciously willed it so.

We have translated "Father" as "Abba," because scholars believe that behind the Greek *Pater* is Jesus' typical form of address for God: "Abba." If we place this prayer in its context, we discover that it involves an expression of surprise and of submission before the divine will, because it is evident that Jesus, like every prophet or preacher, hoped that everyone would accept the message concerning the reign of God in which he so firmly believed. He hoped, of course, that it would be accepted by the pious and the learned, that is to say, by the religious leaders of his people. But Jesus had begun to note with surprise that these were the very ones to reject it, whereas the truth of God's approaching love was perceived by the contemptible crowd, by sinners and the unlettered. Jesus had begun to take note of this, and it surprised him: what was happening was not what he had expected. And it probably pained him as well. But in it he discovered the mysterious will of his Abba, for in this prayer, uttered in public, Jesus submitted himself to that will and gave thanks for it.

Perhaps the most outstanding example of submission to the will of the Abba is Jesus' prayer in Gethsemani, the prayer before the final crisis:

Abba, for you, everything is possible.
Free me from this sorrowful destiny.
Yet let it not be as I will, but as you will (Mk 14:36)

In the first place, as was customary in public prayers, we
find a praise of God—here, a profession of faith in the power
of the Father—preceded by the filial invocation, "Abba,"
dear Father. Then comes the twofold petition. First, concerning his great preoccupation: free me from this fate that
I see coming; save my life. In order to grasp the full force
of this petition, we must realize not only that Jesus was a
young man in the fullness of life, but above all that for him,
in his Jewish humanity, God and life were united: God, the
living and life-giving. Death seemed like a divine vacuum,
the absence of God. Even in the 115th Psalm, which sings
that "whatever God wills, God does" (v. 3), there is the sorrowful note, "It is not the dead who praise the Lord, nor
those who go down into silence" (v. 17). The departed souls
of the just are resting, awaiting their return to life with the
resurrection. He himself had recalled that God had appeared to Moses as the God of Abraham and Sarah, of Isaac
and Rebecca: "God is not a God of the dead, but of the living"
(Mk 12:26–27). But his faith in the final resurrection did not
rob this death-experience of its fearful drama.

Nevertheless, even in the face of the death that threat-
ens him, Jesus submits himself to the will of God: "yet not
as I will, but as you will." In the prayer of Jesus there appear the two elements (the second of them at least implicitly) which every prayer of petition by his disciples should
contain. In the first place, there is the setting forth of some
need of ours that we bring before God—that is to say, we
live in faith; in second place, yet ranking above the first,
there is the desire that God's will be done. Prayer made in
this way always finds an answer on God's part, because in
itself it is already a strengthening and vivifying grace. The
author of the letter to the Hebrews, referring to the prayer
of Gethsemani, says that "God heard him because of his rev-

erence" (Heb 5:7). This may seem strange to us, if we consider that a few hours later Jesus would die on the cross. But on the one hand, God had allowed the Son to die and Jesus had asked above all that his Abba's will be done; and on the other hand, God gave him an incomparably fuller life in the resurrection, so that he became the source of eternal life (Heb 5:9; cf. Acts 3:15).

God-Centered Prayer

Jesus, then, speaks of the prayer of petition as something not only legitimate but also most natural. We can understand why: it obliges us to go out of ourselves, our solitude and our pride. Moreover it supposes faith in the power and love of God. And it makes us relive, in faith, our difficulties. To ask God for something is to feel that one is within the very heart of God.

And yet the prayer of Jesus is centered in God, not in ourselves. He himself told us that we should seek above all the love of God (God's reign) and that all the rest would be added to us (Mt 6:33, Lk 12:31). We have already seen that a saying attributed to Jesus by the primitive church, though not included in the gospels, invites us to "ask for the great and God will give you the small in addition." The "great" is the grace of God, God's reign.

The degree to which our prayer should be centered in God is revealed in the prayer which Jesus taught us and which the church has continued repeating throughout the ages. It has come down to us in two forms: a longer one, amplified for use in the liturgy, that of Matthew (Mt 6:9–13) and a shorter one, which many New Testament scholars feel is closer to the original, that of Luke (Lk 11:2–4). Let us take this latter form as our basis.

> Father!
> May your name be sanctified.
> May your reign come.

Give us each day our bread for subsistence.
(Or: Give us today the bread of tomorrow.)
Forgive us our sins,
for we too forgive everyone who wrongs us.
And bring us not into temptation.

The initial invocation is probably a translation of the Aramaic *abba*, dear father, typical of Jesus. Every public Jewish prayer begins with a divine praise, in this case, "May you be glorified!" (the name is the person). Like Jesus his disciples want the will of God above all things, that is, that God's sovereignty, power and love be acknowledged.

This is followed by a petition relating to both God and us: "May your kingdom come!" This is the central petition, because it refers to the object of Jesus' faith and preaching. Since only God can establish his reign, we are in effect asking: "Re-establish the power of your grace among us." All the remaining petitions refer to the reign of God, if we translate the one concerning bread as meaning the bread of tomorrow, that is, as the full grace of the divine tomorrow, the final messianic banquet. Forgiveness is the preparation for that banquet, and temptation is characteristic of the last days. It is quite possible, then, that the whole prayer has an eschatological content. Nevertheless, it is likewise possible that the petition for bread refers to the relief of our everyday needs: "Give us each day what we need in order to live as your sons and daughters, while we await your grace." This is how it was understood in some manuscripts of Mark and Matthew, and of the Didache (The Teaching of the Twelve Apostles). But even so, this petition is understood as an anticipation of the final grace, for it was well known that at that time there would be no more poor or needy. The satisfaction of our human needs, like the healings of Jesus, announce and anticipate the royal rule of divine mercy.

3

Prayer and Life

It is easy for us to see, in Jesus, how prayer flows from life. His prayer was (historically) and is (for us in the gospel) entirely oriented toward the encounter of his real and living humanity with the love of God. He lived and prayed searching to fulfill God's will, and thus his prayer often consisted in lifting his life up into the mystery of God and in trying to discern God's action in his life. His statement that "not every one who says to me, 'Lord, Lord,' shall enter the reign of heaven, but the one who does the will of my Father" (Mt 7:21; cf. Lk 6:46) only serves to reinforce this conclusion. Jesus reminded us, repeating an oracle of Isaiah, that God does not want to be praised by our lips while our hearts are far away (Is 29:13; Mk 7:6).

According to the traditional definition, the prayer of a disciple of Jesus is a lifting up of oneself, or of oneself with one's conscience, to God. Or perhaps we could restate it more clearly by saying that prayer is a going down into the depths of ourselves to a level where an encounter between God and our own person, life, concerns and relationships can take place. When we pray, we relive our day-by-day experiences in faith, hope and love. For in our prayer, we often thank God for the good times in our past or present life, or express our sorrow for our infidelities, or set our needs or those of our dear ones before God, or try to discern which decisions will best respond to God's love. Our whole real life keeps running like a motion picture throughout the course of our prayer. In fact, even when we try to forget about ourselves and what is happening to us, in order to rest a while in God and simply fix our loving gaze on the one who is more present to us than we are to ourselves, we are still aware of placing ourselves before God in our real being, with our failures and successes, our cares and joys, and we know that the divine glance penetrates into our deepest, truest reality.

Precisely because the reality we encounter in prayer is the infinite and transcendent God, prayer simply has to be *more* than prayer, because God, as we have already said, is not just standing there before us, like one more object among the many objects of our knowledge and our love. God is in each person we meet, behind each object we desire, in the depths of every action we perform. He is God, the inevitable.

Prayer must necessarily be more than prayer. If prayer "is" precisely a meeting and a relating with God, it should be evident that what prayer "does" is simply to raise to consciousness something that is going on in each moment of our existence, because there is not an instant in which God is not present or does not relate to us. Prayer, then, does no more than discover God as the deep ground of our relationships, the last term of our desires, the first source and final goal of our actions. Hence, in order to be authentic, prayer must be intimately united to the rest of our life.

In this connection, it is enlightening to see how the great Teresa of Jesus, in describing each of the degrees of prayer, moves continually back and forth between the way in which believers pray or the experiences they have in prayer, and the way the rest of their life is going. For the fact is that growth in prayer supposes progress in faith, hope and love. And faith, hope and love in turn have to animate and change our whole existence. Hence it is most significant that in the highest degree of the spiritual life—the transforming union—prayer and life become totally fused in an habitual perception of the presence of God derived from that union. Thus culminates a tendency toward the fusion of life and prayer that is in some way present in the very first steps along the spiritual way.

One of the clearest signs for discovering the authenticity or inauthenticity of a person's prayer is its connection or lack of connection with the rest of his or her life. All too often, unfortunately, prayer appears to be something separated from life, whether as an activity that is isolated from all other activities, or as a sort of cozy greenhouse in which we install ourselves. In some cases it seems to be a sort of ritual we have to do out of a sense of duty or because it is something demanded by the good image we have of ourselves or wish to project before others. It also seems that there are Christians who pray on Sundays and totally forget God for the rest of the week. Certain religious give the impression that they pray precisely because they want to be, and above all appear to be, good religious. Yet it often happens that no particular influence of prayer can be noted in their lives.

There are also those people who, because of psychological disturbances or more generally because of problems that impact their psychological balance, seem to live their interior life like caterpillars in their cocoon, aware only of their own experiences, of what they believe they see, hear or feel. Their whole life seems to be concentrated right there. The God whom they claim to encounter (although there can be no doubt that God encounters them) does not seem to draw them out of themselves to the sufferings or joys of the church or the world. There's something strange going on in this sort of prayer. Such people are not to be blamed: it's either impossible or very difficult for them to pray in any other way. Wounded or fearful of being wounded from without, they are incapable of going outside themselves, and thus they hide in prayer as in an emotional refuge. This is, alas, an ideal breeding ground for false visionaries.

Prayer as Remembering

If prayer is a reflective encounter with the God who is in the depths of our being and forms the ground of our life, our works and our relationships, then prayer necessarily entails discovering God's presence in our existence. Or better put, it entails opening ourselves to the God who is revealed in the depths of our being.

We discover God in our past: this gives rise to the prayer of remembrance, of reliving before God our life, with its joys and sorrows. David Hassel, S.J. has presented this type of prayer as an alternative mode of praying.[1] It is more easily experienced by those who have passed midlife, when the past has already taken its toll, including the remaining future they can likely count on. This is the time when saints like Augustine, Ignatius Loyola, Teresa of Jesus and Anthony Claret wrote their autobiographies, discovering God's hand at work in the twists and turns of their lives and giving praise for it. As we read their accounts, we cannot fail to observe the ease with which these friends of God interrupt their narration to address God directly, thanking God for the gifts they have received and repenting of their own infidelity. And although many other men and women have not managed to record their experiences in autobiographical classics, they have in effect done the same thing: they have passed their lives in review before God.

This is the kind of prayer that is practiced, often inadvertently, by a number of widows and widowers, since the grateful remembrance of the love that they experienced forms an essential part of the spirituality of the widowed. The writer of these lines was made aware of this when he heard a homily delivered by a young widow at her husband's funeral, thanking God for the kindness and love of the deceased. Widows or widowers remember the joys they shared with their spouses, the good and bad moments they lived through together, and while they hope one day to encounter the God of the living, and to encounter in God the one they have loved and lost for a time, they thank God for the gift of the person who surrounded them with love here and who loves them now from the fullness of life.

But one doesn't have to be a widow or widower, and one doesn't have to have passed the noonday of life, in order to pray through remembrance. We can all do it, in order to discover God in our past, to rejoice in God's presence and action, and to thank God for it all. In doing this, we reinterpret our life in faith and come to a better understanding of who we are before God. Israel did the same in a number of psalms.

Those who have suffered some trauma in their remote or recent past have a special need of this type of prayer. While one is still reeling under the painful impact of such a trauma, one can only suffer it in prayer. But when one has somewhat recovered from it, it becomes possible to relive it in prayer, to generously forgive those who have wounded us, in the case of an offense, or else to try to rise above that situation. It's not just a question of remembering, but rather one of remembering before God, presenting our wounds to God's healing love. Prayer then becomes therapy: we verbalize our sufferings and difficulties before God in faith and love, with a sincerity that we would never be able to muster in the presence of any psychologist. And we can come out of this experience feeling stronger and freer.

Sometimes the prayer of remembrance comes to us as an unexpected and unbidden grace. Some people, while at prayer, are suddenly confronted with a painful event in their past life and feel invited to forgive someone who has wronged them. God carries out their therapy.

Prayer as Discovery

The greater part of our prayer is projected on the present. It is oriented, consciously or unconsciously, toward discovering the loving presence of God in our present life, or better, toward opening ourselves to that being who is revealed to us as pure grace in our life, here and now. In prayer we repent of our faults of yesterday and today, and we bring God the concerns that are besetting us at the moment. But above all we discover God as the companion who never fails. For a believer, living is always living in company. Although we may not be aware of our companion in the midst of crises and sufferings (*My God, my God, why have you forsaken me?*), we nevertheless submit ourselves in faith, like Jesus, before that mysterious presence.

More often, for those who live in prayer, God appears in the background as the joy and security that nothing or nobody can take away from them. It is like falling in love. We feel filled with inner joy, we skip like adolescents, we feel surrounded by light. In the measure that one becomes contemplative, that is to say in the measure that God brings one into mystical experience, he or she comes to discover God as house and atmosphere: God surrounds them always and everywhere. Or else they discover God as the ground of all being whom they can no longer elude. The fact is, mystics are distinguished for their ability to perceive the irradiation of God in creation or in the history of which they form a part. Mystics are characterized much more by their being able to see everything as animated by a living light than through experiences where the divine reality is "seen" as an object. Many mystics see nothing with their visual imagination, and it is only toward the end that they see some attribute of God (God's kindness, for example) in an intellectual vision. But they are never lacking that loving perception of the presence of infinite love, truth and beauty refracted prismatically in creatures. All prayer prepares us for this discovery.

Prayer as Discernment

It is harder, in fact much harder, to discover God in our future, because the influence of the past that was is still with us. The present is here, within a hand's grasp. But we do not possess the future. For all our dreaming and planning, we don't know what awaits us. Yet we often have to make decisions that are going to shape our future. What, then, are we to do?

Remember that for Jesus, believing means entering into God's future, or, rather, into the God who is our future, because, for Jesus, believing means trusting in the power and goodness of the *Abba*, and submitting ourselves to him. Hence came Jesus' prayer of discernment. Discerning the will of God does not mean trying to find out what God has decided, but deciding in God. Really, without revelation, we cannot know the future God is preparing for us. On the other hand, discerning is not just reasoning, examining which course would be most prudent or weighing the reasons pro and con—although we also have to do that. But, as we already know, God's ways are not our ways, and the logic of the Holy Spirit seems like foolishness to upright and sensible folk. Discernment is an activity guided by faith: it involves walking into the future guided by faith. Discernment consists in discovering what relationship this decision which I have to make has with the love whereby God loves me, with the total salvation to which God calls me, with the vocation God has given me so that I can journey toward God and collaborate in the growth of others. There are some truly worthwhile rules for discerning God's will, especially those given by St. Ignatius Loyola. Nevertheless, the most important thing for us to do is to immerse ourselves totally in God through prayer, so that the decision taken will spring from a will possessed by grace—whether or not the pros and cons of the matter seem to apply.

Praying Within History

It is hard to avoid the impression that those who give themselves to prayer are just bottling themselves up within themselves. For those who have little or no theological or experiential knowledge of mysticism, mystics seem like people who live enclosed within themselves, concerned only or mainly with themselves. That there may have been an exaggeratedly individualist (as opposed to personalist) orientation in spiritual teaching and practice in the past cannot be denied. When a monk who withdrew to the desert refused ordination not because he already had his own—contemplative—way of enriching and serving the Church, but because he was so unsure of his own salvation that he could not afford to be concerned for others, then he clearly showed signs of being influenced by a mentality that does not seem to have come from Jesus or the gospel. A dualist vision in which God and the world are opposed seems to have inspired some of the attitudes of these ancient heroes. We gather the same individualist impression from the vocation accounts of those who seem to have entered monastic life only out of a concern for saving themselves. No one is saved by himself or herself alone. When Evagrius of Pontus identified the reign of God with one's own interior experience, he seems to have given an extremely individualistic interpretation to a symbol which for Jesus was certainly social and historical.[2]

Now what I have just said was not meant to pass judgment on anybody. No. Once and for all, the mothers and fathers of the desert greatly enriched the church. In our times, we too undoubtedly have some highly questionable points of view of our own. But the grace of God always outruns our theologies. We said what we said above simply to manifest the danger that lies in the isolation and uprootedness of a spiritual life that aims at encountering the transcendent God exclusively or mainly through one's own ego. We encounter God in the "I" and the "thou," both in ourselves and in our neighbor. This is what the sacraments are: being reached by God's grace and meeting God in relation to others, through the ecclesial community.

A few times we have heard lecturers say that Teresa of

Jesus seems to have been totally taken up with herself and centered on her own experiences. And we all know that this, if true, would be psychologically unsound. But we suspect that anyone who says this doesn't really know the story of the relationship between God and Teresa or any other Christian mystic. Christian mysticism always entails a prophetic element. The mystic discovers God immersed in history, not only in his or her own history, but in that of the church and humanity, and ends up speaking out in the name of God. When Gertrude experienced the love of Christ, she revealed it to the whole church and modified the course of Christian spirituality. Moreover, in a male-dominated church where women could not act, she made it clear that woman does have an active, ministerial role to play among the people of God. Returning to the case of Teresa, while she certainly had to fix her attention on her own interior experiences, she did so because in an environment rife with illuminism, she did not want to be deceived, and so she wanted to submit those experiences to the judgment of educated and experienced persons. Deep down, too, she did it for fear of the Inquisition, which was not only ever-alert to the spate of false mysticism, but also resentful of those who, like Teresa, had Jewish roots. But Teresa ended up squarely in the thick of history, concerned with the Catholic-Protestant struggles in Europe, with the reform of her order and with the hindrances she met in carrying out her work. And God used her analyses in order to enlighten the whole church. In the long run, she was recognized as a doctor of the church.

The evolution from a pure search for the self to a prophetic re-encounter with the world appears clearly in the case of Thomas Merton. The young Merton looked at his abbey of Gethsemani, at monastic life and at the rest of the world through the eyes of a convert. Grace and salvation were (for him) to be found in monasticism and the world was something that he had simply left behind. Still conditioned by this mindset in *Seeds of Contemplation* (1949), he believed that lay Christians aiming at contemplation (the experience of God) could reach it only by escaping as much as they could from the city: "Do not read *their* newspapers unless you are really obliged to keep track of what is going on." As if anyone who wanted to meet the living and true God could fail to be "really obliged to keep track" of the pains and joys of the world! One of his friends must have pointed out to him the inconsistency of this position, or perhaps the very God he was searching for began to disabuse him, but what is sure is that in the new edition of *Seeds of Contemplation* that appeared in December of the same year, Merton toned-down his words. Ten years later, in *The Inner Experience* (1959), he began to situate the experience of God in the context of daily life, and in *New Seeds of Contemplation* (1962) he stated that solitude does not entail separation, and he stressed his positive attitude toward the world. Shortly afterward, as he was praying in his hermitage under the drone of bombers passing overhead, Thomas Merton became a prophet of peace and justice and discovered a new openness toward the spiritual traditions of other religions (*A Vow of Conversation*). He had come back, in a different way, to the world he thought he had abandoned.

Praying in the Blood of Christ

Since it is impossible to encounter God without encountering his sons and daughters, prayer—every authentic life of prayer—necessarily issues in an encounter with all who suffer. For God is in a special way with those who suffer the most. If every neighbor is an image and a son or daughter of God, those who are oppressed, humiliated, wounded, abandoned, hungry, ignorant, subject to constant insecurity, etc., are so in a particular way. The living God is revealed here to us above all in the oppressed and in the suffering.

It is enough to open the Bible almost at random to be

convinced of this. The prophets protest in the name of God against the humiliation of the poor. But much earlier than they, the prophet of prophets, Moses, discovered God amid the oppression of God's people. For the Hellenistic Jew, Philo of Alexandria and, under his influence, for Gregory of Nyssa and the earliest Christian spiritual theology, Moses was the prototype of the friend of God, of the one who prays in depth. Yet even in the first dialogue between Moses and God that we read of in the book of Exodus—Moses' vocational experience—God appears on the side of the oppressed people: "I have witnessed the affliction of my people in Egypt and have heard their cry of complaint against their slave drivers" (Ex 3:7). We may not exactly know whether Moses saw a bush that burned without being consumed, because the burning bush may well be a metaphor to indicate religious experience. But what is certain is that Moses, in a spiritual experience, discovered the solidarity of God with those who were suffering. Israel, as Archbishop Romero rightly said, is a paradigm of the history of all peoples, be they of El Salvador and Nicaragua, the Philippines, South Africa, India, China, Russia or wherever. In the Bible God sets forth the history of his relations with Israel as a mirror in which we may see the history of all the other peoples of God.

Moreover, as Christians, we know that Jesus, the Son and Messiah of God, identifies with everyone who suffers. This is what the parable of the judgment of nations tells us in Matthew: "Come, share in the blessing of my Father . . . for I was hungry and you gave me food, I was thirsty and you gave me drink, homeless and you welcomed me, naked and you clothed me, sick or in prison and you cared for me" (Mt 25:31–46). St. Thomas Aquinas wrote that the works of solidarity with those who suffer are in some sense a liturgy, because they are done for Christ through the poor[3]—and, we would add, because in some sense they derive from the eucharist, in which we celebrate Christ's solidarity with us and experience his redeeming love.

In the past, Christian charity was limited to taking individuals out of their affliction because nothing else was possible. We would gather up the trash that society flung into the gutter or into city dumps, we gave asylum to the poor who were dying in the streets, to the homeless, to the elderly and to abandoned orphans, but we could not prevent society from converting God's sons and daughters into trash. And Christ rewarded Christians who helped the hopeless. Elizabeth of Hungary and John of God saw the glorious Christ in a poor person. Even so, the fact that Louise de Marillac and her companions stepped out of their life of ladylike ease to live in the midst of a world where sons and daughters of God were suffering was in itself a prophetic (and political) protest against the luxury and indifference of the Court of Versailles. Today it is possible for us to prevent society from converting the image of God into trash. Or at least it is possible to protest, as the prophets of Israel did, against the great machine that converts people into trash, and thus we can have an impact on society, helping both Christians and non-Christians to become aware of the sufferings of Christ in the poor.

It has never been possible to pray without encountering the suffering of God in the sufferings of God's sons and daughters or the passion of Christ in all who suffer. Today's Christian mystic is often discovered with blood-soaked hands. I wrote these words in Manila, a few days before the elections of May 11, 1987. Every day the newspapers and the television told of a number of violent deaths. One cannot pray in such circumstances without becoming aware that the ground we tread on is a holy ground, because it is soaked with the blood of Christ. And like Moses, we have to remove the sandals from our feet.

What relationship does our Christian prayer have with all this suffering in the world? A great and varied one. In the first place, as in the case of Moses, the revelation of God in those who suffer is brought about in prayer. It is in prayer that we become aware that today Christ bears the humble name of Joseph and Mary, unemployed workers living in the favelas of Brazil (Helder Camara), or in the black or Puerto Rican ghettos of the United States, or in the gypsy camps outside of Madrid. In the second place, also as in the case of Moses, prayer is transformed into an impulse that moves us toward solidarity. We should remember that it was in prayer that Martin Luther King and Archbishop Romero discovered their vocation and decided to take action. The oppressed need prophets much more than they need mere activists or professional politicians. And prophets are made only in prayer. In the third place, we intercede in prayer. No, we don't have to pray expressly for all the needy. Even when we don't invoke God's grace in so many words for those who suffer, we are still interceding for them. All we have to do is stand like beggars before God and look at God with humility, or simply to kneel before the crucified, because praying is always interceding.

In some cases, a Christian's persistent prayer turns into keenest suffering. We sometimes go to prayer believing that we will find peace and rest in it; or we go to prayer as to a swimming pool, hoping to find refreshment there. Yet what happens? All the poor of the world seem to jump into the water and stun us with their noisy clamor. Anyone who prays will sometimes experience the sufferings and deaths of far-off people, because they are the sufferings of the crucified who goes on dying in this world. The "nights of the spirit" are often expressly marked by this feeling of compassion.

Prayer from the Heart of the World

The psalms of Israel often burst forth as laments and cries for help out of the very depths of history. There are many psalms in which the poor, the needy and the suffering address God by setting their needs before the helper who can free them from their plight. But there are other psalms that reveal yet another aspect of prayer. There is, for example, a whole series of psalms that proclaim God as the Creator and benefactor of the world. "Yahweh's are the earth and its fullness. For he founded it upon seas, set it upon the nether-streams" (Ps 24:1–2). Hence the world itself trembles before God (Ps 68:9). In still other psalms God's presence enriches the earth with the gift of water and the grain-harvest (Ps 65:10). In this context the human being feels little less than divine, the vizier to whom God has entrusted the governance of all other earthly creatures (Ps 8:6–10).

Prayer is this, too: a praise lifted up to God in the name of all creation, animals, plants, the earth and the stars. Each human being is the conscience and heart of the world. Only a human being can thank God for the gift of living and being. And only human beings can discover God in the depths of everything, as Jesus himself discovered God's caring for the lilies of the field and the birds of the air. Throughout history, some of God's friends have outstandingly fulfilled this vocation of men and women to live in harmony with all creatures, great and small. We think, for example, of St. Francis of Assisi's *Cantico delle creature*, which praises God for "master brother Sun . . . sister Moon and the Stars . . . sister Water who is very useful and humble and precious and chaste . . . brother Fire . . . our sister mother Earth. . . . " It is not at all strange, then, that he who felt the strong bonds of communion that unite us with the other beings in our world should have been described in one of the *Fioretti* as "converting" the threatening (as well as threatened) wolf of Gubbio. Whoever prays feels deeply the family kinship of all the creatures of this world.

John of the Cross, the doctor of God's transcendence and of utter detachment, can find no better way to describe the divine beauty than by attributing to God the beauty of nature itself:

> My Beloved: the mountains,
> the solitary wooded vales,
> the strange and far-off isles,
> the sounding rivers,
> the whistle of amorous airs . . . [4]

When John commented on this stanza and the one that follows it, he was in Granada, contemplating from his monastery the beauty of the night, with the Alhambra in the foreground, listening to the rippling of the water, caressed by the evening breeze. For him, God is the nearby hills, the farther mountains of the Sierra Nevada, the shady valleys through which the Darro and the Genil flow. But God is also the exotic beauty of the distant islands that were beginning to be discovered, from America to the Philippines. John himself comments:

> The strange isles are girt by the sea and lie beyond the seas. They are quite apart and cut off from human communication. And thus there are things nourished and born on them that are different from those that are here; things with strange ways and properties never before seen by men, so as to arouse great wonder and admiration in those who behold them. [5]

The "brave new world" that was just then being discovered would further reveal the mysterious grandeur of God: the plantations, the coconut palms, the fantastic parrots of the Brazilian rain-forest, the strutting peacocks, the immensity of the Niagara and the Grand Canyon, the Amazon and the Mississippi. The whole world becomes a metaphor for the grandeur of God.

Today we have both a broader and more exact knowledge of such things. For Francis and John of the Cross, the world was rather static. Things went on with the same initial beauty God had given them at the beginning of the world. Today we know that creation is a continued impulse through which the plants and animals have gone on to be

transformed and give rise to new forms. God the Creator is
behind it all, giving impulse to and carrying on its development. Everything is moving onward, and we know very
well where it is heading: toward the final appearance of
Christ, the omega and final point of all. Almost in our own
day, Teilhard de Chardin religiously lived this orientation
of the whole material creation toward Christ. His prayer
was converted into a Mass lifted up from the very heart of
the world.[6]

Teilhard de Chardin did not invent this, although he re-
discovered it. The eastern fathers above all had a very lively
awareness of the cosmic meaning of the liturgy. The human
being, for the Greeks, is a microcosm, a resumé of the universe. When Christians celebrate the divine liturgy, the
whole world praises God and is reconciled with God.

Prayer at Work

There are some Christians, contemplatives, whose
task in the world consists of deeply immersing themselves—and with them the church, humanity and the
world—in God. And yet, the first Christian contemplatives,
the fathers and mothers of the desert, discovered very early
on that their vocation in the world also entailed work. They
did not cease being men and women simply by becoming
contemplatives, for they could read in Genesis that God has
put us on this earth to work, and that St. Paul had made it
a rule "that anyone who would not work should not eat" (2
Thes 3:10). They had to pray always, that is, they had to be
like the angels who always stand before God; but they also
had to devote several hours a day to work, in order to support themselves and provide something for the poor. Ever
since then, the Christian monastic tradition has joined
prayer and work. We are still reminded of this by the
Benedictine motto: *"ora et labora."*

Christians know that we have to work. It is our mis-

sion on earth to make the earth more humane by transforming it through work. Our civilization, ever since the
industrial revolution, has been based on work, whether
it be done at a machine, in a laboratory, in a planning
room, in a library or behind a personal computer. But this
work often dehumanizes us. Often we do not experience
it as something that flows from us spontaneously, but
rather as something imposed on us. We have to submit
ourselves to the obligatory rhythm of the organization and
plan that come down to us from above. Houses are often
far from the place of work, separated by one or more
hours of heavy traffic. It's very hard for today's Christian
to find God in his or her work.

For most of us the thought of retiring to some quiet,
rural society, joining some cozy circle of artisans, or taking
refuge in a commune would be nothing but a wildly romantic
dream. Nor does the solution lie, as Thomas Merton proposed in some of his early writings, in trying as much as possible to flee the noise of city life and escape into solitude.
Most of us have to accept the fact of the world of technology
and mass organization. We must try some sort of reconciliation. On the one hand, we have to accept work as an essential part of our vocation, work to support ourselves and
our families, and try to make the earth more habitable for
the sons and daughters of God. On the other hand, we have
to try to find God in our work—not only because God is present in everything, but also because working and producing
are ways of cooperating with the Creator. Believers should
often lift up their hearts rapidly and briefly to God, thankful
for the opportunity to be God's co-workers and constantly
discovering the numberless ways in which God's infinite
love envelops us. Work that is undertaken out of obedience
to the Creator and offered to God in faith eventually becomes a liturgy which, far from dehumanizing us, immensely enriches us. Origen had some interesting thoughts
about it, when he interpreted the biblical invitation to constant prayer as an exhortation to live our whole life and

work as an implicit prayer.[7] Thus our whole life and work become prayer, although not without being oriented by explicit prayer.[8] Simone Weil, the French Jewish thinker who became a worker out of love and suffered keenly the full dehumanization of the proletariat, has left us an example of what a worker-mystic can be.

The solution to the very real problem of maintaining a conscious and loving relation with the God of mystery in the midst of an agitated or at least tiring life does not lie in cutting down on or completely escaping from work (which would be impossible for most people), but in trying to connect, in the mind of our activities, with the energy that flows from God to the world, continuously creating it, "To seek God in all things"—a phrase cherished by Ignatius Loyola—[9] is perhaps the best resumé (better, even, than Nadal's "contemplative in action") of his apostolic spirituality. This need not be understood in what we call a "Franciscan" sense (seeing the face of God reflected in the mirror of all creatures), but in the sense of encountering God in our activity and in our relationships. Although Ignatius Loyola's teaching is immediately applicable in the context of an apostolic spirituality, it has, in fact, a much broader meaning. In Ignatius, in whose "angelic" spirituality religious experience is at once directed toward the operative faculties of the psyche, we encounter a God who is the principle (and end) of all action and work: the God who creates us in order that we may share the divine glory of which the Spiritual Exercises speak so frequently. For the man or woman who works, whether at home or away from home, the Ignatian motto implies encountering the Creator, whose fullness of life and energy penetrates our life and our activity. It means discovering God as the ultimate ground of our intense daily living, and living our work as a homage to the Creator. There is no need to multiply moments of quiet and silence (although it is possible and indeed useful to create some of them in the midst of our busy days); it is enough that we live our productive activity in faith and love.

Meeting God During the Rush Hour

The hours we spend in heavy traffic, in the work-place, and at times even at home, can be among the most enervating moments in our day. Waiting for trains, sub-ways and buses; being surrounded by people who are trying to hide their faces behind a newspaper or a book; driving in a sea of cars and more cars; feeling the bored or irritated glances of those we pass or who pass us; stepping on the brake, the gas, and again on the brake; the daily routine of the freeway or highway—all of these irritants can wear down our will, weary us and set our nerves on edge. Today, when we have given up wearing cilices or flogging our-selves, society has supplied us with new forms of discipline and mortification.

Nevertheless, there are believers who use their rush hours, or at least parts of them, to rest in God's love. Even when we are on the train or in the car or flying above the clouds, we can feel that we are wrapped in the infinite love from which we have come and toward which we are going. God, the silent companion of all our comings and goings in life, can also be with us on the highway. It is a moment we can use to ask God to accompany us through the rest of the day, to thank God for pulling us through another day, or simply to lay our concerns before the one who always loves us.

The very people who are coming and going on either side of us can be an invitation to pray. All we need to do is try to look at them with the love-filled eyes with which God looks at them. Each man or woman is a world in miniature. On the freeway, on the sidewalk or on a train, we encounter all kinds of people, although we may not take notice of them: the young men or women who have just fallen in love (they don't talk about it, but their shining eyes give them away) and keep looking for a telephone; the newlywed, for whom the trip home is still a wonderful surprise; those who are expecting a baby shortly; the woman whose doctor has ordered her to have a checkup and she fears the worst; people who are having problems in their marriages, their work or their children; the divorced and widowed who are walking the path of loneliness; the single who are tired of eating alone before the TV. There are Catholics, Protestants, Jews, along with an occasional Muslim or Hindu; there are some who believe in nothing and others who let their horoscope be their guide. There is a whole booming, pied and motley world of human beings. And God loves every single man and woman of them, even if their only thought is to get back to the peace and quiet of home, to kick off their shoes or loosen their ties. There are some believers who, while they are driving their cars, sometimes try to look with love at all these people—people who are often wounded, always rather tired, and always, always, loved by God. And there are those who sometimes pray for them, thanking God for lovers, for newlyweds, for people starting a new job, for people who are expecting a baby, lifting up to God the painful loneliness of the divorcée or the widow, or perhaps the quieter and more routine loneliness of the single man or woman.

Yes, God is there, even in the midst of the traffic. And it is there that we must seek God.

Prayer and Ministry[10]

Church ministers are painfully aware of tensions between prayer and work. Priests and members of apostolic institutes often complain about how hard it is to pray in the midst of a life dedicated to intense activity. Today these tensions are felt even more keenly in view of the functional/productive, almost "industrial" interpretation attached to ministry. We have to "do" a lot, we most often have to work in an institution (parish, school, hospital, chancery), we spend long hours planning, meeting and coordinating calendars that are jam-packed with activities. We usually set off early in the morning and get home tired in the evening.

The apostle-mystics have taught us, by their lives more than by their words, that the solution does not lie in the way of limiting activity. There have been genuine mystics—from Francis Xavier to Louise de Marillac to Anthony Claret—who worked intensely throughout many long years. Naturally, all of them were careful not to let their activities, at least ordinarily, rob them of the prayer-time they needed in order to nourish themselves through God's presence. However, they did not seem to be overly concerned if once in a while they had to miss the time they had set aside for prayer, so long as they had to leave it in order to serve God in their neighbor. And they were richly rewarded with the gift of experiencing God's presence in the midst of their ministry.

The important thing is to accept our ministry in obedience to God, who calls us to it, and to accept it with a firm decision to help our brothers and sisters to find God's grace—not looking to ourselves or to our own successes. Often enough our failures are more effective than our victories: that is the mystery of the cross. Anyone who works in obedience to his or her vocation to be humble instruments of God's grace accepts the privations, wearinesses and failures that crop up in their ministry. Anyone who works with the poor or the oppressed, anyone who tries to make God's grace present in families divided by lack of love, alcohol or drugs, anyone who serves desperately ill people or loveless elderly people, can do no less than suffer with them. These things are an essential part of apostolic asceticism. St. Paul gives us an outstanding example of all of them: "It is not ourselves we preach but Jesus Christ as Lord, and ourselves as your servants for Jesus' sake" (2 Cor 4:5); "Continually we carry about in our bodies the dying of Jesus" (2 Cor 4:10); "Leaving other sufferings unmentioned, there is that daily tension pressing on me, my anxiety for all the churches. Who is weak that I am not affected by it? Who is scandalized that I am not aflame with indignation?" (2 Cor 11:28–29).

But Paul resorted to prayer and invited his fellow Christians to join him in it: "I beg you, brothers and sisters, for the sake of our Lord Jesus Christ and the love of the Spirit, join me in the struggle by your prayers to God on my behalf" (Rom 15:30). Prayer is an essential part of apostolic service. We pray for those we serve, even when we don't mention them expressly, because we immerse ourselves in God and God enriches us through them. We need to revive, in prayer, our concerns, our works, and the sufferings and joys of those we serve. But above all we need to immerse ourselves in God's loving presence, in order to radiate it to others. And we radiate love to others to the extent that we ourselves feel loved by God.

From this starting point, the apostle-mystics have left us two great lessons. Fr. Jerome Nadal, speaking of St. Ignatius Loyola, calls him a "contemplative in action."[11] Like him, we must strive to encounter God mysteriously present in the very midst of our service, to try to live immersed in God while we are working for God. But we must admit that this formula doesn't express the whole of the matter. St. Vincent de Paul was closer to the mark when he recommended that what we need to do is *"être passifs dans l'action"*—to be passive in action[12]—which means to let God be God in us, to let God work through us. This is what Ignatius Loyola, Vincent de Paul, Madeleine Sophie Barat, Catherine McAuley, Anthony Claret, Don Bosco and others did. And so did the great Paul who—like them and like us—bore the treasure of God's grace in an earthern vessel (2 Cor 4:7).

4

The First Three Degrees of Prayer

The way we pray keeps changing throughout our life in the measure that we ourselves keep changing. Today as never before in history, we have become acutely aware of the fact that every human life involves series of periodic deaths and rebirths. Our life is a succession of cycles or seasons. We reach a degree of balance and maturity in one, and all too soon new questions and new points of view arise to destroy the balance we have reached and force us on to seek a new balance. Throughout the various stages from childhood to adolescence to adulthood to middle age to old age, we move on, struggle, adapt and are transformed in the process.

Since these changes are so deep and all-encompassing, they are necessarily reflected in our prayer. Why? Because praying is relating ourselves to God, and every relation changes if even one of the members of the relationship changes. We ourselves change and so do our images of God. James Fowler has shown that just as our image of the world and of ourselves in the world keeps changing throughout the various stages of our life, so does the way in which we image God.[1] Children, adolescents and adults tend to place themselves differently before God. Moreover, another part of passing from one cycle to another is a sense of malaise and unrest, which goes far toward explaining a number of related crises in our prayer life. Spiritual directors can never afford to overlook the particular life-situation of the persons who are talking to them about their encounter with God in faith.

But the prayer of a believer tends to be transformed throughout his or her life at a far deeper level and in a far more radical manner, for reasons that have nothing to do with the psychological development of his or her personality. There is a transformation in prayer that is due to purely spiritual reasons. We refer to those believers who are making an effort to follow Christ faithfully, and who therefore, like Christ and with Christ, open themselves up to the presence of the *Abba* in their lives and become increasingly aware of God's presence in their individual prayer life. In the measure that they allow themselves to be invaded by this presence, their religious experience becomes fuller and more radical, and they begin to notice that their prayer is expressing itself in forms and modes of which they had previously had no inkling—and all of this quite independently from the stage of life they happen to be in. Thérèse of Lisieux and Elizabeth of the Trinity were both very young when they died, yet Thérèse had time to go through a harsh dark night of faith and Elizabeth had enjoyed some very high spiritual experiences even when she was an adolescent. Edith Stein reached great spiritual maturity without going through a mid-life crisis. On the other hand, the majority of believers run through the various stages of life without ever managing to get out of the most rudimentary forms of prayer. The reason that we are dwelling on this point is that it is not uncommon nowadays to note a confusion between psychological development and spiritual progress. For instance, despite the many similarities that might be drawn between the "mansions" of Teresa of Jesus and Carl Jung's phases of personality development, the tendency to peaceful interiorization, which is reflected in the prayer life of an adult who is approaching middle age, may have nothing to do with the infused recollection which in the Teresian scheme serves as a stepping stone to the fourth "dwelling place."² Of course, this does not mean to imply that this period of interiorization and integration does not bring with it a marvelous opportunity for a new form of prayer that may prepare us for the graces of infused recollection or mystical quiet.

There are many stages in the itinerary of prayer, from the first approach to God in spoken prayer all the way to full mystical union. Moreover, as St. John of the Cross observed, the changes that occur in prayer and in the experiences that accompany it are marked by special nuances and appear in diverse forms in each individual. That is why St. Ignatius Loyola laid such great stress on the duty of paying constant attention to the way God is moving the human spirit. But for all these differences, human being remains essentially the same. Hence, the fundamental outline of all the ways of prayer tends to be essentially the same. Naturally, individuals who share the same spiritual and temporal tradition will have more elements in common, yet even so there can be great differences among them. Think of the differences that separate Thérèse of the Child Jesus from Sister Elizabeth of the Trinity, although both of them were contemporaries, both shared the same middle-class French background and both became Discalced Carmelites.

The Causes of Progress

From what we have just said, one can already guess the factors that lead to the development and transformation of prayer within us. They can all be reduced to one: the grace of God. Prayer is a divine gift which grows with God's grace. The cause of progress in prayer is, therefore, "outside" us, in God. Grace is translated into faith, hope and charity. And here the reason for it is in God and in ourselves at the same time, because faith, hope and charity are gifts of God, variations or effects of grace in our several faculties, but they are now a welcomed and received grace, a grace that transforms us. Prayer is not a reality in itself: it is simply the expression of faith, hope and charity. Praying is expressing our faith, our hope and our love. Hence, when these virtues become more intense and begin taking greater possession of our faculties, prayer develops.

It is a well known fact that faith, hope and charity—or, more radically, the grace of God—develop in us to the measure that we open ourselves to grace and allow it to possess us. This is (to steal a phrase from Paul) the obedience of faith (Rom 1:5). We grow by submitting ourselves to God's will in our manifold activities and in the various zones of our lives. For this reason, there is no better preparation for prayer and for making progress in prayer than the fulfillment of our vocation, the humble service we offer every day at work, at home or in our social relationships. This is something that laypersons and those who are called to the apostolic life must bear in mind. Loving obedience to God in our family (however we define "family") or in our ministry is a factor for our growth in a life of prayer. This doesn't necessarily depend on the time we devote to prayer or the psychological techniques we make use of at prayer, but, rather, on the intensity of our love. We pray in the measure that we love.

But prayer forms part of the program of any man or woman who is a disciple of Christ (of the gospel) in the same way that prayer was incarnated in Christ's own life. We are all called to live our relationship with God in a conscious way, and not just to offer the service of our activities. Our service entails prayer. Moreover, prayer is a necessity. Those who love have to express their love. Those who want their whole life to be open to the Spirit will have to maintain a conscious and lively relationship with the Spirit. Times for prayer, whether in common or in private, are necessary. Their frequency and length will depend on the vocation of each individual. These times of personal prayer will help us live the rest of our life with God and in God. Prayer-acts lead to habitual union.

The Goal

Every life moves on, passing through transformations toward its fulfillment. All roads lead to a goal. The outer goal and the inner way give meaning to all our journeying and living. It would be well for us, then, to ask what is the goal that gives meaning to our prayer life. And the only answer is: the same goal that gives meaning to every Christian life, because prayer is nothing more than an aspect of Christian life. The goal is reached in the last stage of that life, the stage of full love, where life and prayer are at last completely fused. That is what they have been tending toward throughout the whole process of development.

From the outset, Christian tradition has attempted to describe this goal from different points of view. An exposition of these attempts, however brief and sketchy, will give us a better understanding of this final stage of fulfillment and, by that very fact, of the development of the life of prayer.

Communion with Christ in the Church. For Paul, "the" apostle, prayer without ceasing (which he commends so highly: 1 Thes 2–3; 2:13; 5:17; etc.) is no more than an important aspect of the new life in Christ which we receive in faith and which the Spirit imparts to us in baptism, making us sharers in the fruits of the paschal mystery. We pray as sons and daughters, because we bear within us the Spirit of the Son. Hence in Paul's own experience, reflected in his letters, our communion with Christ and the action of the Spirit in us appear in bold relief. But there is an equal stress on our solidarity with the rest of the church, the community of those reborn to new life, the body of Christ, into which we are introduced, as members, in baptism. We pray with one another and for one another. And we feel the burden of all the churches.

Return to Paradise and Angelic Service. For the earliest contemplatives—the fathers and mothers of the desert (fourth–sixth centuries)—the goal of Christian living and of prayer is twofold: a return to the paradise lost of our original vocation (Adam and Eve conversing familiarly with God) and an anticipation of the life of the blessed: unceasing prayer, a service rendered to God which makes us like the angels, who always stand in God's presence. Benedict (sixth century) understands community prayer as a public service to God, centered on scripture reading, and he speaks of individual prayer as the fruit and continuation of the former. Monks and nuns (Christians) are above all menservants and womenservants of God in the church.

Re-Creation and Vision of the Divine Image. The fathers of the church seem to stress the idea of a return to our original condition by way of interiorization. Christian life tends toward the progressive restoration of the divine image within us. Through a spiritual ascent, the eyes of the soul are opened and the soul contemplates God in the divine image which the Spirit has re-created in us: a contemplation which is at once luminous and obscure (Gregory of Nyssa, Gregory of Nazianz). Hence in Augustine the way of the spirit is a process of entering into ourselves until we encounter God, three and one. All of the fathers speak of ecstasy (standing outside the sensible world), joy and peace, as characteristics of this vision.

Spousal Union. In commentaries on the Song of Songs, in which the bride is taken to represent the Christian person, the fathers of the church sketched the first notions of a nuptial mysticism that would be developed in the west by the writers of the twelfth century, great medieval women mystics (the two Mechtilds, Gertrude, Hadewijch) and formulated by John of the Cross (sixteenth century) in his Spiritual Canticle. The whole spiritual way is a going out in search of the word, the Son of God, a purification and preparation for union with God which will become a definitive marriage (two in one Spirit). It should be recalled that not only in Latin and its daughter languages, but also in German and its cognates, "souls" is a feminine term. Moreover, given the interior status of women in the societies where these writings flourished, the bride or espoused woman was perceived as a suitable symbol for the Christian person, while God was cast in the role of husband or bridegroom. One consequence of this imagery was that it tended to give a rather feminine cast to the spirituality of a number of men.

Re-Encounter with the Being of Beings, Beyond all Things. The theoreticians of Rhineland mysticism, Eckhardt, Tauler and Suso (fourteenth century) returned to the fathers and their Christian Neoplatonist heritage, using a more metaphysical vocabulary. God is being; the creature is nothing. God communicates being to creatures continually, so that he constitutes the ground and source of their very being. For them, the whole spiritual way consists of despoiling oneself of everything that is not God, in order to become united with that primordial being. Contemplation leads us to discover, in the deepest depths, the God who is above all. From Augustine and the Rhenish and Flemish mystics, Teresa of Jesus inherited a view of the spiritual life as the soul's gradual entering into herself until she reaches the most deeply recessed dwelling place, where God dwells. In that innermost chamber, the spousal union takes place. God, to her way of thinking, is the Lord ("my King," "my Emperor," "His Majesty") who lifts up his lowly servant to the rank of spouse.

Communion in Service. Some twelfth century writers, as well as Teresa of Jesus in the sixteenth century, experienced the drive to action that springs from mystical experience. The nearer the soul draws to God, the greater violence it feels to do and suffer for God. Mystics called to the apostolic ministry, such as Ignatius Loyola (sixteenth century), Vincent de Paul (seventeenth century), and Anthony Claret (nineteenth century) have experienced and described the final stage of their journey as a full communion with Christ in which prayer and ministry are fused. Ignatius was set alongside the Son in an attitude of service. Elizabeth of Hungary (thirteenth century), John of God (sixteenth century), and Vincent de Paul saw Christ in our lords, the poor. Anthony Claret could not contain the charismatic violence of his apostolic zeal.

This is the goal, described in varied and fragmentary ways, by those whom God brought to this final stage. We can find no better description of it than a collage of all these descriptions. From the moment individual believers begin to address themselves to God with filial love and meditate on the mysteries of Christ, they already know where their prayer is heading: toward making them live their life fully in Christ for the good of the church and of humanity; toward returning to them the paradise of innocent grace; toward contemplating the image of God one and three in the depths of the soul; toward standing like angels before the face of the divine mystery, in humble service; toward entering ever deeper within themselves in order to transcend themselves; toward being united with infinite love; toward experiencing the violent yet gentle power of the Spirit. May God grant this to us all.

Point of Departure: The Word

It would probably not be out of place for us to turn back and comment on a point we made in the first chapter: at the root and source of all Christian prayer we find the word of God. God, we remarked, initiates our prayer by creating us and revealing the divine self to us in our own history. By "word," we meant the divine word, using a concept taken from the scriptures. But in these scriptures—given their semitic world view—the "word" means a great deal more than it does for us westerners, who tend to think of a word as a mere sign that transmits a concept or feeling. In the Bible, "word" also means "action" or "event"; it is full of energy. "God *said*, 'Let there be light!' And there *was* light." This might also be translated by saying that God acted, or intervened, and light appeared. When it is said that God speaks in Israel, it means that God made the divine self present, and acted, in order to save the chosen people. The divine word is always creative and redemptive: a word that springs from God's infinite mercy and is hence a grace (hesed). For this very reason, "word" can mean an event in which the presence and action of God is discerned. In the gospel according to Luke, we are told twice that Mary, the mother of the Lord, "kept these words (events) and pondered them in her heart" (Lk 2:19 and 50). Hence, in the Bible, "hearing the word" means being open to the divine presence and action, letting them transform our person and life. In this connection, it is interesting to note that whereas Mark and Matthew speak of "doing the will of God" (Mk 3:35; Mt 12:50), that is, of opening oneself to the saving will of God, Luke translates "hearing the word and putting it into practice" (Lk 8:21; 11:28).

Jesus, the Christ, is "the word made flesh" (Jn 1:14), because in him God is made definitively present and active in our history. The letter to the Hebrews touches on this notion when it states that "in the past God spoke to our ancestors at many times and in varied ways through the prophets, but in these last days, he has spoken to us by his Son" (Heb 1:1–2). Revelation, therefore—God's self-gift to us—reaches its end-term in the Son of God. Nothing further than this can be said or hoped for. St. John of the Cross was wounded at the fact that people should have recourse to prayer in order to seek further revelation: "In giving us His Son, His only Word (for He possesses no other), He spoke everything to us at once in this sole Word—and He has no more to say."[3]

But though the divine self-gift has come to us objectively in Christ, that grace continues to give and communicate itself to each one of us. The latter is related to the former, because to each man or woman the divine Spirit applies grace, the fullness of which resides in Christ. And in each man and woman, the Spirit evokes the *memoria Iesu*, the remembrance of Jesus, of the way in which God has saved us in him, of the way he lived his faith in the divine reign and communicated this faith to others. God continues speaking to us, although God now speaks to us by way of remembrance, explanation and application. God does this in many ways: through others, in the ecclesial community, and by inner movements. But in a unique way God does this in the inspired scriptures, both of Israel and of Christianity. In them, God recounts the long history of God's own love for us. This is why the reading of scripture is an essential part of the church's worship.

In Christian monasticism, *lectio divina* (literally "divine reading" or reading of the divine word) has always been regarded as the beginning of every community or individual prayer. The fathers of the church insisted on the individual reading of the scriptures. We find them speaking of the "two tables," namely the table of the bread of the eucharist and the table of the bread of scripture, or, if you will, of the one table of God at which Christ is offered us under the guise of two forms of nourishment. For the fathers and for the great writers of the Middle Ages, this was not simply a matter of devotional reading, but of something far more fundamental, because the word of God that has come down to us in the Bible is the word that creates, redeems and transforms us. By reading the scriptures, we submit ourselves to the word and action of God.

Thus, very early in Christian tradition, there was a stress on the need to chew and ruminate on the divine word, that is, to savor it, apply it, digest it and assimilate it. This theme appears in the letter of Barnabas (second century), in Clement of Alexandria (third century) and in the literature of the desert fathers and mothers (fourth century). Later it is commented on by Augustine and Isidore of Seville, and reappears in William of St. Thierry (twelfth century) and even in the *devotio moderna*, a Flemish-Rhineland spiritual movement of the fourteenth and fifteenth centuries.

In Christian tradition, then, all prayer life begins in reading and receiving the word of God and constantly returns to it. Every prayer is a response to the word received.

Reciting, Meditating, Feeling

We are going to begin our description of the itinerary of prayer through its first three stages, the first of which (recited prayer, sometimes less aptly called vocal prayer) is common to all who practice even the basic minimum of religion. People recite prayers in public worship and many do so even in private. We are going to dwell rather insistently on these first three phases, since part of our aim is precisely to help others surpass them and thus dispose themselves for contemplative prayer.

We have called these first three stages "reciting," "meditating" and "feeling," respectively. Recitation is the repetition of a traditional formula or of a prayer written by someone else. Meditation consists of a slow and deliberate reflection on, say, a biblical text, some mystery of the life of Christ or some event in our own life—a reflection which usually leads us to address God, or gives rise to some affective reaction in us. By "feeling," we mean a kind of personal and interior prayer which is predominantly affective and in which the psyche expresses its love, joy, sorrow, etc., before God.

Someone may ask whether we are dealing with three successive stages here. The answer is, "yes and no." "No," because these ascetical forms of prayer (called "ascetical" because it is the human individual who produces them under the sway of God's grace) depend a great deal on the various types of personalities who are praying. Some types who are incapable of discursive meditation may pass from recitation to affective prayer, or may even be led by the Spirit from recitation to a divinely infused (mystical) prayer. In other types, affective prayer may either not appear at all as a separate state, or may do so only in the most tenuous form. On the other hand, we could answer "yes," they could be considered as three successive stages of prayer, because these three forms often follow one after the other. We all begin with recitation, which is the most elementary form of prayer, the prayer of the uneducated or barely educated, and the prayer of all those who for one reason or another do not get beyond it. Meditation requires a greater capacity for introspection and reflection, and many devote themselves to it once they begin to give themselves over in a systematic way to personal prayer. Finally, affective prayer usually appears unexpectedly in a number of people who have heretofore not gone beyond meditation, yet do so upon reaching maturity, with the sudden outburst of the feminine, intuitive, affective, relational side of their human nature. In others, in whom the feminine side is predominant, meditation is rather early converted into affective relationship.

The First Degree: The Prayer of Recitation

The first stage along the way of prayer is characterized by an overall predominance of the recitation of formulas received from the community. This is what is ordinarily called vocal prayer, that is, prayer pronounced with the voice. But the important thing here is not the fact that spoken prayer is predominant, but that prayer in this first stage consists precisely in the repetition of prayers not created by oneself but learned by heart or read from a written text. What predominates, then, is the use of particular word-sets and formularies.

Note that the distinction between vocal prayer and mental prayer is not a very precise or even good one, if by vocal prayer we mean prayer that is merely pronounced orally and by mental prayer we mean prayer that is performed within the mind. St. Teresa of Jesus observed that unless a prayer arises from within, it can't really be considered a prayer, whether it is uttered by the mouth or not.[4]

In contrast, the distinction between spontaneous prayer that we ourselves create and prayer that we in some way take over from others is very important, in the sense that the predominance of spontaneous prayer, together with the more or less constant absence of rote prayer, usually marks the transition to a new stage of the spirit. Those who tend to limit themselves to praying in received formulas establish a minimal contact with God by splitting their attention between God and the formula in their memories or on the page before their eyes. The more these formulas are repeated or prolonged, the harder it becomes to focus on the words themselves, which tend to fade into the background of a general and respectful consideration of the one we are addressing in recitation.

Recitative prayer is predominant among two main classes of persons. In the first place, it is predominant among rather uneducated persons who are not accustomed to rising above the level of the concrete. In the past, whereas priests, religious and the educated laity were taught how to interiorize through meditation, the unlettered majority of Christians were taught how to recite numerous devotions. But even aside from this, we can speak of the predominance of recitation, the repetition of prayers, together with that spontaneous sort of dialogue that forms a considerable part of the prayer both of very active or extroverted people, or of those who are much more affective than reflective. In either case, whether the difficulty is imposed by society (insufficient instruction) or by temperament, this greater or lesser predominance of recitation is no obstacle to the believer's being lifted up by the Spirit to higher degrees of prayer.

The second class of persons whose prayer tends to be limited to recitation is made of those believers who have in fact given up further developing of a personal prayer life, ordinarily after having cultivated one for some time. These are usually priests or religious who, during their years of formation, learned to interiorize and personalize their relationship with God through meditation, but later abandoned it and fell back on celebrating the eucharist without any living, inward participation, and perhaps on reciting some part of the liturgy of the hours, or eventually on reciting some popular devotions with the faithful who attend their church. The liturgy is, to be sure, much more than a public recitation of formulas. This is true, in the case of the eucharist, not only because it is a sacramental action (the action of Christ through the community of his disciples), but also, on the human side, because of the times of silence, music, and atmosphere it includes, and the synthesis of interior attitudes and bodily expressions it presupposes. The liturgy is a most effective means for progress in the spirit, and, hence, in prayer. But one can clearly be reduced simply to acting in the liturgy, without allowing oneself to be led by the word and grace of God. It is also clearly possible that those who do not cultivate a personal life of prayer may in the end come to the deadening state of limiting themselves to a mere "performance." Those who have given up on developing a personal life of prayer, yet are forced by their vocation to confront the living God in community prayer, are often attacked by remorse. But in some cases, all remorse seems to cease. The life of prayer doesn't seem to be for such men or women.

The Second Degree: Meditation

Meditation has traditionally been understood not to mean just any form of interior or mental prayer, but that form of individual prayer in which reflection predominates. Those who meditate usually take as the object of their prayer a truth of faith (heaven or sin, for example) or an event from the life and passion of Christ, which they recall and reflect on, or rather "contemplate" in the Ignatian sense of the term, by entering into the scene as if they were witnesses of the actions and words involved in it. The greater part of the meditation refers to God or Christ in the third person. It is not then so much prayer to God as it is a prayer about God. But all the spiritual masters insist that this reflection must issue in affections and dialogue, that is, in prayer properly speaking. One thus comes back to establishing the kind of I/Thou relationship initiated in vocal prayer and which is typical of biblical religion. But now this relationship has been internalized and deepened. The believer first takes up the word of God, from which the truth of faith comes or is embodied in the mystery that is meditated on, applies it to one's own self, throwing light on one's own existence, and responds to it with one's own affections of love, gratitude, reverence or sorrow.

From what we have said thus far, it should be clear how important this stage of life of prayer really is. In former times, from the seventeenth century on, writers and preachers used to speak of the usefulness of meditation to reform our lives, that is, to maintain and better our fidelity to the gospel. Hence meditation was strongly connected with an examen of conscience and, from the time of St. Francis de Sales onward, was always expected to issue in some particularized good resolution. Meditation certainly leads us to better our lives, and resolutions are always good (though often ineffectual), precisely inasmuch as they are a manifestation of good desires and a petition for God's grace. Today, with our less spiritualistic and voluntaristic anthropology, we are aware, on the one hand, that the decisive forces guiding our lives are not just our decisions and, on the other, that our emotions and feelings are of very high worth.

We would say that the stage of meditation is very important because it sets up the basis for the successive development of the life of prayer—and that, for several reasons.

Above all, there is the deepening effect of meditation. It tends to give us a deeper grasp, in an attitude of faith, of the mystery of God's grace revealed in Christ Jesus. The believer takes, for example, some stage in the life and passion of Jesus, attentively reads a gospel text or a commentary on it, runs it like a videotape through his or her memory, contemplates Jesus, tries to intuit his motivations, reflects on his mercy or his patience, etc. There is certainly more to this than a mere exegetical study (although such a study might be very useful as a remote preparation for prayer), but there is also an attentive reflection on the text or story that is recounted. The believer enters more deeply into the object of his or her faith or love.

In the second place, this reflection on God and divine grace, from a viewpoint of faith, strengthens and nourishes the praying person's relationship with God. As we already remarked, this meditation on God should issue in addressing oneself to God. Meditation never deals with abstract truths, but with a personal Being: God, Jesus, Christ the Son of the living God, God's love for us, God's patience with us, etc. We gain a better knowledge of the one we wish to love. We become more familiar with the Spirit of the Lord.

In the third place, meditation brings about an interiorization and deeper rooting of our faith. The word of God is received within us, mulled over, savored and applied to our person and our life.

Finally, this deepening, interiorizing and relating makes it possible for the deep psyche to go about its secret work of summoning up and forming images of God, the all-source, of the Son, and of the life-giving Spirit. We arrive at the next stage of prayer with certain images of the heavenly world, produced under the influence of our environment. Personal meditation will help us to shape our own perception of the divine reality and its dealings with us. We will experience God in the very way we need to. We will discover God's patience or mercy or generous grace or truthfulness and fidelity. We will instinctively select those traits of Jesus that best serve to increase our friendship with him: his prayer, his commitment, his compassion, his dealings with women, his proclamation of God's forgiveness, his mysterious sufferings, his glory and heavenly intercession. Gradually a more powerful image of God and of Jesus' humanity will emerge in the depth of our psyche. In the past, under the influence of Alexandrian Neoplatonism, the Christian mystical tradition showed a haughty contempt for our "phantasms" on God, urging us to develop a purely spiritual kind of contemplation, since God is beyond all our fantasies and imaginings. This approach was on the wrong track, because, even though all believers cannot fail to be aware of the infinite distance that looms between God and their images and ideas of God, they must, until God brings them into the darkness of contemplation, open up the inner world of their fantasy and sensibility before God.

These images, which the word/grace of God keeps shaping in our psyche, are powerful symbols that are going to attract and channel our spiritual energies. Around them, our spiritual experiences are going to anchor our deepest appetites: our desire to love and be loved in our true identity, even with our limitations and failings; our hunger for truth and authenticity. An image of God/love is going to animate our relationships not only with God, but with ourselves and with others. From the next stage on, there will be moments in which these images will explode into affections. In some individuals they will later erupt beautifully into imaginative visions that accompany God's action in them. Now, perhaps, we can better appreciate how important meditation is during the early stages of prayer life.

From the seventeenth century until Vatican II there was a growing over-insistence on meditation, rigidly structuring it and often converting it into a predominantly intellectual exercise. This was doubtless done under the influence of an idea of human nature in which reason was vastly overrated. It reached the point where it was thought that someone could go on meditating until death, and the restless were invited to follow this royal road, without presuming to strike out on the (dangerous) roads of other, higher forms of prayer, unless, of course, God should push them in that direction (e.g., Rodriguez, *The Practice of Perfection*). Allied to this tendency was a middle class, orderly and methodical understanding of the spiritual life, together with a fear of incurring the church's anathemas against quietism, or of falling into the snares of the Illuminati, who were being hotly pursued by the Inquisition.

But the fact that the importance of meditation was exaggerated in the past, converting it into almost the only form of mental prayer, should by no means be taken to mean that meditation has lost its usefulness in certain stages of the spiritual life. We have already pointed out the reasons for its continuing usefulness. Today, to be sure, there are many more possibilities for interiorizing the word of God than there were in the heyday of the vogue for meditation. There is much more preaching today; the celebration of the liturgy in the vernacular is a great help; there are prayer groups where people can reflect on passages from the Bible, etc. Nevertheless, we believe that a certain period of reflective prayer is most useful for those who are beginning to give themselves over to personal prayer. We listed above (we repeat) some of the reasons that lead us to believe that this is so. We would now add that this type of prayer responds admirably to the basic attitudes of those who find themselves at the end of adolescence or in the first years of adulthood. Hence it is highly commendable for students preparing for the ministry (ordained or otherwise), for younger men and women religious and for young persons who are beginning to devote themselves to personal prayer. Naturally, this reflective prayer can take many forms, from meditation properly so-called (reflecting on a gospel passage, for example) to contemplation in the Ignatian sense (taking some incident from the life of Christ and trying to participate in it by setting oneself in the scene as an onlooker). The important thing is that the image of Christ, his values and his ideals, be gradually interiorized.

The Third Degree: Affective Prayer

In meditation, the predominant factor is reflection by way of the understanding. All one need do is to read through the various "points" given in the classic meditation manuals to realize that although the whole process should issue in salutary affections and desires, a good part of the time is dedicated precisely to an intellectual consideration of the assigned topic. We have already seen that, from the time of Francis de Sales on, it was considered necessary to end the meditation with a concrete resolution. In other words, to the work of the understanding, there was now added the decision of the will. Moreover, prayer came to be associated with an effort at conquest, aimed either at reforming one's own life or at being more effective in the apostolate. What we had, then, was a very masculine interpretation of prayer. It is significant that St. Francis de Sales began to change his notions on prayer after he became familiar with the mystical experiences of St. Jeanne-Françoise Frémyot de Chantal. But aside from this, it must be admitted that in meditation properly so-called, a predominant role is played by what Carl Jung has called the *animus*, the masculine side of human nature: reflection, analysis, penetration and transformation of reality, decision.

Nevertheless, there comes a moment in the spiritual itinerary of prayer when reflective activity begins to change into a loving gaze and the psyche is kindled into outpourings of affection. The one praying finds it easier and more spontaneous to feel than to think: sometimes with affections of joy, sometimes with affections of sorrow, but always with love—sentiments of gratitude, repentance, humility, or simply admiration for God's grandeur. The feminine side of the psyche, Jung's *anima*, plays a predominant role in prayer. The *anima:* relationality, affection, feeling for life, savoring of wisdom.

Sometimes, even for those who don't seem to have had much success with prayer, who have not committed themselves to it intensely and have thus not established a strong or deep relationship with God, meditation will tend to cross over into affective prayer. Today, most of us are aware of that period in the life of an individual, that decisive stage in the process of personal integration, when the ignored or repressed side of the personality tends to emerge and impose itself. This repressed side is what Jung calls the "shadow." When it emerges, many men begin to encounter their feminine side. Many celibates who have lived more by decision and work rather than by feelings begin to feel the release of their affective side. This is reflected in prayer. Reflection and consideration are succeeded by affective contemplation. It is time to change attitudes in prayer. One has to allow one's affectivity to give vent to itself. This can also be a period of integration on the level of faith.

There are other times, however, when this transition is not a matter of the individual's psychological evolution toward a phase of integration in which the forgotten self is revindicated. Sometimes the appearance of a predominantly affective type of prayer is the effect of the development of prayer and spirituality itself. Living familiarly with God in prayer leads to an increasingly friendly relationship in which sentiments begin to gain in power. And this can happen even when the individual is far from reaching that stage of adult life where the forgotten part of the psyche comes to light. Note that we're not talking about those feelings that often appear rather easily in those who are beginning to commit themselves to prayer, feelings which the ancients used to call *sensible fervors*. The feelings we are talking about are more powerful, more passionate and more characteristic of adults.

Someone who has reached this level of prayer tends perforce to change reflective meditation into a more intuitive and concrete consideration. He or she may be moved by an incident or even a single verse of scripture and needs nothing more in order to enter into communication with the Lord, turning this incident over in his or her mind, or repeating this verse. One possibly effective help in this degree is the so-called "Jesus Prayer," which originated among the monks and nuns of the Christian east: a reverent and affectionate attention to Christ while one repeats the invocation, "Lord Jesus Christ, Son of the Living God, have mercy on me a sinner." The titles of Christ or, as Fray Luis de León would have said, the "names of Christ" may be changed in keeping with the liturgical cycle or gospel incident which serves as the point of departure for one's prayer.

Christ in the Prayer of His Disciples

Near the beginning of this chapter we observed that Christian prayer is continually nourished by the scriptures. But we also noted that for Christian faith, Christ himself is the word of God in a unique manner. The Christian scriptures proclaim him, who died and is risen for us. And his disciples, since the earliest days of the church (cf. Lk 24:26–27), have regarded the scriptures of Israel as being oriented toward that final revelation of grace in him.

The prayer of disciples must be "in Christ," that is, made in communion with him, under his inspiration. If Jesus prayed to God as his *"Abba"* (Mk 14:36), Paul affirms that the proof we are sons and daughters of God is the fact that we in the Spirit (or the Spirit in us) cry out "Abba" to God (Rom 8:15; Gal 4:6). And the letter to the Hebrews describes the glory of Christ as a constant intercession for us. For a Christian, praying always means uniting oneself to the prayer of Christ in glory. We always pray with him, whether we know it or not.

Meditations on the Life of Christ, once attributed to St. Bonaventure, speak of prayer as "dwelling with the Lord."[5] Whoever prays, we would add, dwells with Christ—and this in two senses: because those who pray are close to Christ, who inspires them to pray (Christ on earth), and because those who pray are together with Christ who prays for us in glory (the one who prays, in heaven). This is a reality that should be consciously lived from the very first steps of vocal prayer. Teresa of Jesus has said as much in some very beautiful words on reciting the Our Father: "Since you are alone, strive to find a companion. Well what better companion than the Master Himself who taught you this prayer? Represent the Lord Himself as close to you and behold how lovingly and humbly He is teaching you. Believe me, you should remain with so good a friend as long as you can."[6] "He wants us to remember Him often when we say the prayer, even though because of our weakness we do not remember Him always."[7]

Jesus, who is our teacher and companion in vocal prayer, becomes, in meditation, the object of our reflections. While the fathers reflected frequently in their writings on the life, passion and glory of Christ, western writers, beginning in the twelfth century, begin to write "meditations" on him. In his Spiritual Exercises, Ignatius Loyola devotes the Second and Third Weeks, as well as the start of the Fourth Week, to meditating on the life, passion and glory of Christ. And it is well known that the Exercises are a condensation of the whole spiritual journey. Here, too, one always walks with him, meditating on him.

The presence of Christ is not limited to ascetical prayer, whether discursive or affective. The presence of Christ is sensed in mystical experience, because it is from the fullness of his grace that we receive grace upon grace (cf. Jn 1:16). In her earlier years, Teresa of Jesus accepted the dictum of certain Neoplatonizing theologians who held that after reaching a certain point one should leave behind the humanity of Christ and immerse oneself in the divinity.[8] It is known how the Christian mystical tradition has been often in tension between the demands of a spirituality of total transcendence of time and visible realities, such as requested by Neoplatonism (today the request comes from Buddhism) and the Christian statement about the role and presence of Christ. The Neoplatonist request arrived through Pseudo-Dionysius (Syria, fifth century) to the Rhineland-Flemish spirituality and from there to certain books read by Teresa of Jesus. Throughout her life she felt that it had been a betrayal of him.[9]

Teresa's experience was confirming the other tradition affirming the permanent presence of Christ in the mystical stages of growth. Origen has already presented the union with the word of God as the goal of the spiritual itinerary. For Gregory of Nyssa, Christ is at the same time the heavenly tabernacle in which we must enter to converse with God and the rock into whose cleft we must enter to contemplate God:

> We say, then, that Moses' entrance into the rock has the same significance as these descriptions. For, since Christ is understood by Paul as the rock, all hope of good things is believed to be in Christ, in whom we have learned all the treasures of good things to be. He who finds any good finds it in Christ who contains all good.[10]

Later Bernard followed by Guerric of Igny will see the wounds of Christ in "the clefts of the rock in which the beloved, as a dove, takes shelter."[11] And John of the Cross will return to the rock who is Christ as the place of the mystical experience.[12]

Not a few of the highest mystical graces received by disciples are graces of communion with Christ. Sponsal mysticism, cultivated mostly by women, sees the transforming union as a state of spiritual marriage with the Son of God. Francis of Assisi received the stigmata of Christ, Simeon the New Theologian was called by Christ his friend, brother and co-heir, and Ignatius Loyola was placed "next to the Son."

5

Prayer and Crisis:
The Crises of Prayer

Our lives, we are told, develop in a zig-zag pattern. From time to time we come to a turn and have to change direction, if we want to go on living fully. Looking at it another way, we can compare our life to a series of level planes stacked one on top of the other. We are walking rather easily along one level stretch, when suddenly we have to make an effort to get up to the next level. The path of life stays on this steep plane until it once again levels off. Sometimes these turnings or ascents provoke a full-blown crisis, such as those of puberty or middle age. At other times, however, as in the passage from late adolescence to young adulthood, the change seems smoother and it arouses fewer emotional storms.

There are other sources of crisis in our lives: failures at work or in the ministry, difficulties with friends or members of one's own religious community, the discovery of marital infidelity or an inability to understand one's spouse, exhaustion from overwork or from the routine character of our work, etc. Often enough these forces conspire with the lifestage changes we described above, for example, those that typify midlife crisis. But they can also come upon us at midpoint between changes. We can all experience failures at work or become exhausted from overwork at any moment in our life.

Obviously, all these crises affect our prayer life. In

some cases, when the crisis relates to a lifestage change, a new form of relating to God may result from a new way of seeing the world of God, and of seeing one's self in God. The adolescent leaves behind the prayer of the child, and shapes for himself or herself a mode of prayer in which, as in his or her own world, conscious interpersonal relationships are highly valued. The boy or girl encounters a God who reaffirms them in their own being, understands them and strengthens them in their search for values. In that case, God can become the decisive other in their lives and evoke a powerful commitment on their part. Those who work in youth ministry know a great deal about this.[1] The longstanding, committed presence of churches in the field of education has led many ministers to become real experts on the subject. Since the process of prayer life that we are studying most often begins in late adolescence or in mature adulthood, we do not plan to dwell on the prayer life of adolescents.

On the other hand there are other crises whose consequences for our prayer life have received little attention until recently. The first of these we would like to refer to is the "midlife crisis," with its difficulties, wearinesses and the transformations that are at work during it.[2] The second would be the crisis caused in women by the cessation of the fertility cycle, with the great biological and emotional revolution it entails. Until the present, there has been little reflection on the spiritual side of this crisis, which is only now beginning to become evident. The reason for this ignorance is very simple. Until a short time ago, only men were spiritual directors and women did not feel inclined to confide in persons who, because they were male and celibate, had little familiarity with this feminine reality. The problem has at last begun to emerge fully in the confidences women now share with other women in the course of spiritual direction.

The Crises of Prayer

Our prayer can undergo crises for reasons intrinsic to prayer itself or, if you will, to the development of our faith, even when we are not biologically or psychologically in crisis. We can be enjoying life, experiencing no serious problems in our relationships and having great success in our work, and at the same time be undergoing some more-or-less deep crisis in our interior life. We periodically go through spells of aridity when we find it hard to concentrate on our prayer (although we may be able to concentrate very well on our work), while the affective part of our relationship with God seems to have dried up completely.

The witnesses of the Spirit show a clear awareness not only of these periodic crises in the life of prayer, but also of their causes. They are all crises of growth. The most serious of these crises are rooted in the development of our personal faith. To the degree that our contact with the mysterious reality of God becomes more intimate, the images of God that we relied on in the past tend to disappear. We experience more powerfully the transcendence and sovereignty of God. Our theologies die away and we find ourselves, like Moses, in the dark.

The First Tests

A period (or periods) of dryness often seems to occur rather shortly after we begin to devote a set time to individual prayer each day. Most people who are just beginning to walk in the way of prayer find certain joy in it. New ideas of God keep welling up within us, we begin to fix our glance on God, we enjoy moments of peace, and it looks as if we're getting better control of our lives. But there comes a moment when everything seems to come to a standstill. We are still capable of reflection, of course, but as we find no real taste in this exercise, our memory begins to grasp at the

most disparate bits of information. If we try simply to concentrate on the presence of God, we find it terribly hard to
do so. In both instances we have lost the feeling of the presence of God that had given meaning and strength to our
prayer. Our fidelity is being put to the test. And indeed, the
important thing at a time like this is to remain faithful. This
dryness (or drynesses) that we feel at the very beginning
does not mean that we should change our manner of prayer,
or that we have exhausted its possibilities. If we persist in
seeking God above all things, the freshness will return to
our interior life. An important recourse for us during these
first trials is the support we get from a group or from our
spiritual director's invitations to persist in praying. These
tests usually don't last for a long time. They are simply the
typical ups and downs of beginners.

Prayer of Dryness and Boredom

Although this description may be applied to all periods of spiritual aridity we have described, we are using it
to refer especially to a rather long phase of development
during which the believer feels lost. It can come on after
years of individual prayer of any type (discursive, affective,
centering, etc.) and can go on for some years. We all go
through it in one way or another if we persist long enough
in dealing personally with God.

In not a few cases, it may coincide with midlife crisis,
but in most cases this crisis of prayer comes earlier and is
due to the development of prayer itself, and not to biological
or psychological causes. What this means is that any form
of prayer characterized by the activity of the believer (no
matter whether it is reflective or affective) has ceased to be
the ordinary prayer of the person involved. All efforts at
meditating or expressing affections are useless. The Spirit
is preparing such a person for deeper forms of prayer. The
prayer that our will and our understanding had heretofore

been making has simply petered out. The mystics tell us that at this time the soul is being prepared for a stage in which God is going to do the praying, and the soul is going to feel as if it is passive. We should note, however, that in this context the term "soul" does not mean (as it did in classic psychology) the conscious part of the psyche. The prayer we are talking of springs from much deeper regions of our being. This is a perceptible phenomenon. The human being is going to feel invaded by powerful forces that spring from within.

The really "bad" thing about this prayer of dryness and boredom is the fact that those who are going through it can't find themselves in any identifiable place, whether in their activities, their ideas or their affections—the last of which have become both few and weak. And they haven't yet reached that experience of passivity we referred to. They are not in themselves and they feel no hint of being in God. Unfortunately, many get lost at this point and abandon prayer. "Nothing's happening," they often say. Even when they don't abandon prayer, they can put serious obstacles in the way of the Spirit's action by straining to pray as they used to, that is, by active meditation.

The name we've given to the phase we're describing— the prayer of dryness and boredom—may have struck several readers as odd. It may seem odd, because this phase is perceived, by those who are actually undergoing it, precisely as a lack of prayer rather than as a form of prayer. It always strikes them as being something purely negative, and not as a higher degree of prayer. The greatest dissatisfaction or pain of those experiencing it comes from the feeling that God has withdrawn from them and from the suspicion that this may be due to their own faults.

This may indeed often be the case: prayer can dry up for a while because of our sin. But this has to be clearly understood, because prayer is never a reward for our good works. If this were the case, no one would make progress along the paths of prayer. On the contrary, the gift of prayer is given to us in order to purify us. Not a few Christians know by experience (and among them Teresa of Jesus) that the faults we commit out of weakness are not an obstacle to personal converse with God, but that they can, on the contrary, spur us on to repent and to petition God for help.

But our failings, those which we commit almost inadvertently, are one thing, whereas our attachment to evil inclinations is quite another. The latter can indeed dry up the roots of prayer. It can happen that we refuse to offer God something that the Spirit is asking of us. We pray, but we don't want to hear what the divine word is repeatedly telling us. The flow of prayer is checked. Most often we can go on praying in a formal way, but we don't allow prayer, or rather faith, hope and love, to penetrate us in depth. We go on semi-deliberately committing faults (faults against charity, against truth, against humility), although we are fearful of committing the graver sorts of sins. We are and we aren't; we knock at the door but don't want to go in. Then comes this stagnation in prayer. It bothers us because it reminds us of our situation, so we take refuge in a purely ritual form of prayer. Personal prayer becomes rarer and rarer.

This period of dryness can become something negative, even when the causes just mentioned are lacking, if the person suffering it begins to leave off praying or to be very inconstant in it. The Spirit of God lets us distance ourselves, like a mother who allows her children to go just so far before she calls them or even drags them back to herself. It is a well-known fact: God's patience is our salvation. But so long as the individual flees from prayer, his or her state is rather negative. He or she may still have the advantage of one remaining benefit: the experience of his or her own frailty and inconstancy.

A Dead-End Street

Let us reflect more on this painful phase of prayer where the believer seems to be standing in front of a high and impenetrable wall. Constance Fitzgerald has applied to this condition the notion of an apparent impasse or dead-end street.[3] We have the impression that we can't go any further. We either turn back or stand still, staring at the same wall, the same banal objects. There's nothing banal about them. In fact, these same objects of religious reflection, these same activities and relationships, are going to burst forth with light. But for the moment they seem banal enough, because we have exhausted one way of looking at them and experiencing them.

It should be noted that in life itself, these situations of impasse occur periodically when, as Belden Lane once wrote, "our customary way of acting and living reaches a dead end."[4] This is exactly what we are talking about here. Our way of praying or reflecting on God in faith suddenly issues into a dead-end street. Later, reflection will be replaced by a simple intuitive gaze, but for the moment we are not yet accustomed to this way of relating with God.

We frequently encounter this dead-end phenomenon in interpersonal relations, including those we value most highly. Our understanding of the other person seems to run out, our feelings grow dull and we don't know how to get out of the mess we're in. Something like this happens to us during this crisis of prayer: our habitual manner of relating to God seems to be heading nowhere. Here, too, a wall seems to have loomed up between our ego and the other. And our concept and images of God don't respond to anything or produce any echo within us. All that is produced is our incomprehension of God and God's ways. We are tempted to doubt the worth of prayer and a kind of skepticism attacks us.

But although the experience of crisis in our life and our most valued interpersonal relations can throw some light on what is happening in this crisis of prayer, it does not offer us an adequate understanding of the phenomenon, because the spiritual life has distinctive characteristics all its own, and our relationship with the mystery of God is marked by some utterly unique traits. St. John of the Cross, who focused carefully on these painful experiences, regarded them mainly as purifications. Anyone who commits himself or herself habitually to prayer, he tells us, experiences joys and consolations; hence he or she tends unconsciously to pray in order to seek this contentment and not simply to seek God. Moreover, this constant dedication to prayer tends to produce a certain sense of self-satisfaction. Prayer thus tends unconsciously to be perceived as a work of our own through which we feel justified. Both tendencies and several more (no one has surpassed John of the Cross in analyzing the vices of spiritual people) are directly combated by what he calls "nights," because in them all consolations are brought to a sudden halt, and the believer experiences his or her own spiritual powerlessness. And, we would add, the kind of prayer he or she had become used to is now over and done. If we pay careful attention to this analysis by St. John of the Cross, we will find that this is undoubtedly an instance of a first purification of love. We had been tending to seek God through his gifts and ran the increasing risk of loving God's gifts rather than their divine giver. We were seeking God, yet were tending to search for ourselves, our own justified conscience, our own refined pride.

This night is really caused by the exhaustion and closing of one (discursive) way of addressing God, and the opening-up of a new way, which John of the Cross calls, even at this stage, "contemplation."[5] It is in essence a confrontation with the present yet transcendent God beyond concepts and images. Many people who have committed themselves to personal prayer and have experienced this dryness find it hard to identify their experiences with what St. John of the Cross tells us. Nevertheless, the Spanish mystic notes that "the sensory night is common and happens to many."[6] Speaking of people who have committed themselves more decisively to serving God, he states that "this usually happens to recollected beginners sooner than to others. . . . Not much time ordinarily passes after the initial stages of their spiritual life before beginners start to enter this night of sense."[7] What they feel most forcefully is the absence of their old way of prayer and the drying up of their affections. Many of them make an effort to go on praying as they used to, which only makes them more acutely aware of this absence and this dryness. During this period, only a few remain tranquil and wait on God's good pleasure with faith and humility. The many others we spoke of either turn back or remain in painful stagnation.[8]

Self-Contentment and the Experience of Powerlessness

Various reasons seem to conspire to convince us that we should persist in making "our" prayer, the kind of prayer to which we had become accustomed. The first of these reasons is of a spiritual, or rather anti-spiritual, nature: the prayer that we are making produces a certain sense of contentment with ourselves. We feel the satisfaction of doing something for God or of fulfilling a duty. This refined pride is difficult to uproot, because it doesn't look like pride, but like a legitimate feeling of assurance that we are on the right path. And what better proof of this could there be than our being able to make "our" prayer?

Hence, the great usefulness of the sense of powerlessness that invades us when we can no longer make "our" meditation or our affectionate dialogue with God. The believer now *feels* impotent, powerless. This is a great grace of God, because here, precisely, is the beginning of our salvation. In the lives of God's friends there is usually some experience which we might call one of overthrowing or undoing. God destroys the project they had formed for themselves and their future, before grace begins to reveal to them his plan for them. Francis of Assisi was imprisoned and fell sick. Ignatius was struck by a cannonball that broke his leg. The sickness and imprisonment of the one and the wound of the other sent their military dreams up in smoke. When Elizabeth Ann Seton's young husband died in an Italian *lazaretto*, she was led to place herself totally in the hands of God.

Here, in this experience of powerlessness that sooner or later strikes anyone given to prayer, we find something similar. For we begin praying in the belief that prayer is something we ourselves can do, and we end up realizing that this was an illusion. Since God's grace was sustaining us imperceptibly, we derived something from it which we somehow attributed to our own good will. But now it seems that God's grace has left us, and we realize that we can do nothing. In reality, God's grace has not left us. Quite the contrary. We are being given a higher grace. What happens is that what this grace produces is precisely darkness, distaste and dryness. St. John of the Cross tells us that these "nights" do not come from a lack of light, but rather from an excess of new light for which we are not prepared and which leaves us blinded for the moment.[9]

God acts like a mother. Remember what happened to us as children. Mama sent us to wash our hands before dinner. Naturally we wanted to do it ourselves, because we were big now, not like a baby in the highchair who had to have everything done for him. We would go to the bathroom, and instead of washing our hands, we got soap all over us. Finally mama came and interrupted our game, and standing behind us dried our hands herself. Then we came out clean as snow. The comparison is clear: we persist in thinking we are adults, capable of many things in the spiritual life. Mother-God sends us to wash our hands, and we spend years at our ascetical games, all the while taking ourselves very seriously, until we realize that we are still quite dirty. When we realize this and turn our eyes like beggars to God, our mother who is in heaven will come and make us truly clean. "Wash me and I shall be cleaner than snow," said the psalmist (Ps 51:9).

The second reason we resist leaving "our" prayer behind is the fear of finding ourselves in a situation we can't control. We like to control everything. Isn't it characteristic of adults to be able to control their situation? While we are busy in the midst of our ideas, examinations of conscience and resolutions, it seems to us that we are in a rational and controllable world. Beyond this, we fear, lies a world of feelings, powerful emotions and indefinable experiences which, according to the mystics, we can't control. Some people—both men and women—have spent a lot of time developing a "virility complex." They have been busy shaping their own image with purely "virile" traits of ideas, decisions and actions. To these men and women, any mention of religious affection smacks of sentimentalism. And they mistakenly tend to reduce mystical experience to sentiment.

Finally, another reason has been explicitly given for remaining in the prayer that we ourselves make. It is of a theological or rather pseudo-theological nature. In prayer, we have to ask for things, examine our lives and make concrete resolutions. All of this presupposes that we have to remain very active in prayer. In answer to this oft-repeated difficulty, Fr. Baltasar Alvarez, S.J., a confessor of St. Teresa during six of her most formative years, came out in defense of an attitude of being passive and entrusting oneself to God in prayer. In it, although a number of concrete practices of virtues may not be done, a great deal is done by simply resting in God,[10] and although the person may not be asking for concrete things for the church and for particular persons, "in a certain way more is asked without asking, by simply being silent in the presence of God."[11] Let us put it another way: we obtain more self-reform, more energies for the apostolate, and more intercessory power by experienceing God's love for us than we do by many resolutions and petitions. Those who pray by letting God pray in them are seeking God rather than seeking to be enriched by God's gifts.

Abandoning Personal Prayer

It seems that a certain number of people, after cultivating individual prayer for some years, abandon it. They may be laypersons, caught up in the busy whirl of life, or they may be religious or priests. Some laypersons, after making a retreat or cursillo, or being in contact with some charismatic group, have in fact made a decision to devote, if possible, a short time every day to individual prayer in the solitude of their heart. But later, the busy train of life, their family life with the comings and goings of its members, or yet other reasons, lead them to give it up. Religious in formation and seminarians have had to commit themselves to prayer, more or less out of conviction, by dint of their environment. In doing so, they were helped by the rather discreet example or control of their peers or their formation directors. Then come the years of harsh daily reality, and the practice of devoting a certain time to individual prayer each day begins to fade until it becomes just a memory. We have said *each day* (taking into account that there may be days when one can't set aside such time), because unless we ourselves make the commitment to place ourselves in God's hands each day, our prayer will begin to slack off.

But what are the motives that lead a person to abandon individual prayer? The fact is that while fidelity to prayer has but one foundation, namely, love of God, there can, on the contrary, be many motives for abandoning prayer.

Ethical Motive. Perhaps there are many who imagine that prayer is only lost through our sins. This is the view held by certain Catholic circles. Certainly, the abandonment of prayer usually coincides with an awareness of our own spiritual powerlessness. We see ourselves beset by faults and failings, and we see them in our surroundings. We begin to suspect that we're not the stuff that saints are made of. We lose (thank God!) our over-confidence in ourselves. But we also lack one very important thing: trust in God and faith in God's merciful grace. We have already remarked that our sins cannot hold God back. We might even say that God reckons on them. Our faults don't matter to God, so long as, on the one hand, we are sorry for them and, on the other, we accept them with humility. But this is precisely what we are lacking: a tranquil and joyful awareness of our imperfections. Our faults are humiliating to our self-love and we don't want to remember them. Or else we believe that we have to be terribly clean to deal with God and, not being able to reach this terribly clean condition, we begin to flee from God as constantly and even more effectively than Jonah did.

Psychological Motives. The motives based on our psychology are more varied. One of them has its origin in a person's temperament, and is therefore of a psycho-physical nature. Some people are bursting with energy and find it very hard to attain the inner quiet needed for prolonged prayer. Personal prayer calls for such a great effort on their part that they are attempted to abandon it. Others are extroverted, little inclined to inwardness and fond of socializing. In both cases a great deal could be gained by a little self-control and above all by finding the form of mental prayer best suited to their temperament or personality type. But as a good deal of effort and constancy is required in both cases, the temptation to abandon prayer may win out in the end.

There are people who, for one reason or another, don't seem able to get in touch with their own feelings, perhaps because they don't want to face some of them and have become accustomed to repressing them. These people also seem to have a hard time cultivating friendly relationships with God. They may be rather cerebral types who have few friends and tend to convert meditation into a purely abstract consideration which they have a hard time giving up. In general, those who don't communicate generously with others, are unconcerned about others and don't "make friends" have a much harder time cultivating prayer.

Environmental Motives. Sometimes our life, the relationships we form and the occupations we follow seem to conspire against frequent personal prayer. Laypersons often find it hard to set aside time for personal prayer. Many have to be on the run early in the morning, work all day, and return home worn out after their struggle with the traffic; or else they reach the end of the day exhausted from household chores and then have to face the comings and goings of the rest of the family. Religious and priests seem to be more favored in this respect. After all, aren't they occupied with the things of God? Listening understandingly to other people's problems, helping confused people find their way or encouraging others to have faith and trust can, doubtless, be a spur to one's prayer life. But if a ministry is performed without looking attentively to the Lord who is present in our lives and the lives of those we serve, it can turn into an alienating experience. Young religious and priests often plunge into their activities with such gusto that they seem to find their highest self-fulfillment in them. Physical and psychic energy, as well as the joy of being both useful and loved (substitutes for fatherhood or motherhood) seem to keep them going. Older religious and priests may find themselves simply ground down by the dizzy pace of their days.

Spiritual Motives. Finally, there are the insidious and in some cases more decisive motives that come from mistaken spiritual attitudes. The most harmful of these is the search after prayer for its own sake, and not for the God of prayer. There is often a certain idolatry of prayer. There are plenty of people who talk about it or tend to boast more or less subtly about it. It is often remarked that those who talk most obsessively about sex are usually the ones who don't lead a sound sexual life. Something similar can happen regarding prayer. Of course, if someone has received the gift of prayer from God, he or she can't help showing it at least indirectly. But there seem to be others who are all too prone to talk explicitly about it. This quest for prayer for its own sake is in reality a quest for oneself for one's own sake, and not a search for God and for oneself in God.

There are others who don't boast about their prayer, but seem to have embarked on prayer more or less hoping that God will speak to them by way of certain experiences. They are really not looking for God but for their own experiences. As God cannot be manipulated and doesn't show up for the appointment, they abandon prayer, instead of simply asking God humbly to change their hearts.

Finally, some mistaken attitudes arise from a kind of ignorance. There are people who from the very outset seem unable to discover the mode or method of prayer that is most connatural to them. They wear themselves out flailing about uselessly in the dark. Others have doggedly devoted themselves to meditation for years. But for all people who have faithfully practiced meditation, the time inevitably comes when it doesn't seem to do them any good. The believer either finds it impossible to meditate (and this is a good sign, as we shall see), or else his or her meditation becomes a routine and arid exercise which brings no living encounter with God. Is that all we can look forward to? In these cases, too, we often hear the disconsolate refrain: "Nothing's happening." And one is tempted to abandon prayer, rather than simply trying out a new attitude or a new mode of prayer. Anyone can see that many of these failures could have been avoided if the person had been able to rely on a spiritual confidant or on an experienced and knowledgeable director.

6

Waiting for God

Many—perhaps most—of those who reach this phase of the prayer of dryness or boredom don't know how to behave in it. What is there for them to do, when nothing's happening? Discursive meditation doesn't take them very far; their affections have dried up. And God seems to be absent.

What To Do?

The only answer to the question "What to do?" is simply, "Nothing," if by "to do" we mean "to perform some particular activity." One doesn't have to "do" anything, because neither the attempt to meditate discursively nor the effort to express affections will be of much help, but may rather cause no small amount of harm.[1] Still less will straining to repeat prayer after prayer, heaping up words, do anything to resolve the difficulty. But if, on the contrary, by "to do," we mean "to adopt an attitude," then the answer to our question is twofold: (1) remain faithful to daily personal prayer; (2) keep waiting for the grace whereby God is going to transform our life and our prayer. Both can be summed up in a single response: keep waiting faithfully for the grace of God.

We have already said that this boring dryness is a great grace. God is very present in this critical phase of our spiritual development—more actively present, in fact, than when we had such clear ideas and such facile affections.

What is happening to us is that our faculties of perception are facing the void that remains after God has deprived us of our ideas and feelings and before we have been filled with the divine presence. We did not have an adequate perception of God, either through the ideas we formed about God or through the images around which we centered our affections. All of this has disappeared now, leaving us alone in the void. Later we will realize the terrible inadequacy of all we had clung to. The passive nights (and that is what we're dealing with) are not due to a lack of light, but to an excess of light that leaves us blinded until God accustoms our eyes to it. Perhaps it would be better to say that what the Spirit of God is preparing for us is an intuitive perception, in which we "sense" God in the depths, with our whole soul, and not simply as an "object of our reason."

Now there's nothing for us to do but wait and watch for this new coming of God in the light. What else can we do, seeing that we can no longer "make our prayer"? Just wait while the Spirit of God does her work in us, praying with groans unutterable, until we ourselves at least come to an awareness of God's praying in us. For we can't even hasten the coming of the light. It will come in due time and in due manner: God's time and God's manner.

Mary and Lazarus

An image comes to mind: the image of Mary of Nazareth after the annunciation, Mary in her Advent, her time of hoping and waiting. In her, the expectancy of a pregnant mother becomes a prototype of our waiting for God. We have to wait as grace grows within us, pay loving attention to the hidden presence within, and (as the old meditations used to say in their interpretation of Mary's visit to Elizabeth) busy ourselves with works of love for our neighbor. Nothing can more effectively prepare us for enjoying God's love than loving our neighbor.

In reality, our expectancy is not exactly that of a pregnant woman who is already carrying within her a new life, because, in the final analysis, that new life is something that she has engendered, whereas in this matter of deep prayer, we are doing nothing but disposing ourselves and above all letting God dispose us—and in the meanwhile, waiting. Therefore, upon the image of Mary in waiting, we have to superimpose, like a transparency, the image of the beggar Lazarus. Lazarus, too, watches and waits, but he is waiting outside for some crumb of compassion from the rich man seated at a banquet table inside. In the glory of God, Christ is celebrating his banquet with his men and women friends. The light of divinity is nourishing them. We are outside, covered with misery. All we can do is wait until the door is opened and the grace of God falls our way. This reinterpretation of the parable has one point that needs to be clarified. In the case of the rich banqueter, he was the one who kept the door opened or closed. In the case of God and Christ, we are the ones who keep it closed. The gate will be opened when we are ready. We have to be patient, not with God, but with ourselves, imitating God's patience with us.

The humble yet hopeful image of the beggar appears in the writings of Teresa of Jesus where she is trying to describe the attitude of the person who has reached this phase of the inner journey: "First, in this work of the spirit the one who thinks less and has less desire to act does more. What we must do is beg like the needy poor before a rich and great emperor, and then lower our eyes and wait with humility."[2]

Saint Teresa of Jesus was deeply convinced of how much patience God shows in dealing with us. Writing to her sisters, she tells them not to

> become disconsolate if you do not respond at once to the Lord. His Majesty knows well how to wait many days and years, especially when He sees perseverance and good desires.[3]

Both images—that of Mary awaiting the birth of Christ and that of the beggar Lazarus awaiting the rich man's compassion—point to the same thing: a Christian must live in hope.

Prayer and Hope

Hope defines the very attitude of the believer toward God. Christian faith is hope, because it leads us to submit ourselves to a God who has not yet been fully revealed in each of us, to the God who is our future. We hope for the glory of God; we hope that God will sustain us with the divine grace so that we may reach this glory.

In very few situations is the eschatological orientation of Christian existence toward the final consummation revealed so clearly as it is in this phase of the life of prayer, because what the believer needs here is to hope. He or she must remain faithful to personal prayer, guided by faith amid the darkness and sustained by hope. And what is the believer hoping for? Revelations? Revelations of what? asks John of the Cross. Hasn't God been completely revealed, once and for all, in the Son, the eternal word? "He spoke everything to us at once in this sole Word—and He has no more to say."[4] Neither does the believer hope directly for divine favors. The believer hopes in God and waits for God. God suffices and more than suffices for our littleness. But waiting for God means hoping that God will give us the grace of a more intimate and intense relationship in faith. And this, in the opinion most commonly held today, brings with it mystical experience. Later we shall see that mystical experience does not essentially consist in having imaginative visions (more often, in fact, it is unaccompanied by them), but precisely in an experience of God's loving and active presence within us. This experience is a fruit of the development of the gifts of the Holy Spirit, and these are given to all in baptism.

We keep waiting hopefully for God, knowing that both God and God's gifts will be revealed to us. It would not be too much for us to insist on this. We don't have to be looking for prayer, whether high or low: we have to be looking for God. The former could be a kind of subtle idolatry. It would be making prayer an end, whereas its end should simply be hoping in God.

The Prayer of the Poor

Let's get back to the idea of praying like a poor person waiting to receive an alms of grace. We have all frequently witnessed the silent patience of beggars on the streets of our great cities. Not too long ago, as I was walking along Market Street in San Francisco, I saw a young man sitting on the curb on one side of the street, and a woman sitting almost directly across from him on the other side. Both were young, probably in their thirties. Their faces were lined with sadness and they kept their eyes down, fixed on the pavement in front of them. Both held cardboard signs that indicated their needs. His sign read: "Be kind to me. I have AIDS." Hers read: "Help me. I'm pregnant and homeless."

These sad experiences throw some light on the situation of those who have remained faithful to prayer during more or less long periods of dryness. The experience of their own misery doesn't reach a clearly conscious level at the beginning of this period of spiritual dryness. Although they are afraid of having lost the ability to pray because of their sins, which now seem to be more frequent and considerable than they had previously thought, there comes a moment when they begin to feel their own misery more intensely during prayer and at the same time feel moved to place themselves in God's presence in an attitude of patient waiting. This was what happened in the case of St. Teresa's Jesuit confessor, Baltasar Alvarez, when he was a young man.

After years of meditation, he began to see that it was getting him nowhere: "For sixteen years I worked at it like a man plowing but not reaping. . . . After fourteen years I was put in the position of placing myself in the presence of the Lord, waiting for an alms like a poor man."[5]

It was in the nature of a passive experience. He felt moved by the Spirit to this prayer of presence and silent, patient petition: "I was put." He began to have this experience after fourteen years of apparently useless efforts at prayer. The spiritual aridity continued, but the servant of God had learned from the Spirit not to wear himself out trying to express himself through his faculties, but instead to remain in the presence of God in a humble and silent attitude. He himself believed that this same way of prayer could be recommended to persons who are "very weak of head, who may well enter and begin here, even though they are very near the beginning."[6]

Needy Creatures

What happened to Baltasar Alvarez is practically the same as happens to all believers who reach this stage of purification and persist in prayer. At this time they become aware of the fact that before God we are doubly in need: as creatures we totally depend on God as the source of our being, and as sinners we totally depend on God as the source of the grace whereby we live. In these persons, prayer becomes a humble, and silent, petition.

"Asking God for what is fitting for us" ("*petitio decentium a Deo*") is precisely—together with dialogue with God and lifting up our soul to the divine mystery—one of the three traditional definitions of prayer.[7] We might have spoken of it in the first chapter, when we dealt with the other two definitions, but we have chosen to defer it to this phase, where the need of it is more powerfully felt. We have already remarked that Jesus always refers to petition when he speaks of prayer, as if all we had to express to God were our needs, rather than our admiration for God's grandeur, our praise for the divine glory and our acknowledgment of God's benefits. This is all the more striking in view of the fact that in the gospels Jesus himself sets us an example of other types of prayer, such as the prayer of wonder before the mysterious designs of his Abba and of submission to them (Mt 11:25–26), or the prayer of complaint and conformity (Mk 15:34). Curiously enough, when St. Thomas Aquinas deals with prayer in the *Summa Theologica*,[8] he centers it on the prayer of petition. St. Bonaventure tells us that any prayer that did not deplore our misery and ask for grace would be imperfect.[9]

In reality, all of this should not surprise us when we bear in mind that all prayer, even that of glorification and praise, is at depth petition. The reason is, of course, that before God we cannot cease being what we are in our very root-condition: totally dependent and needy creatures confronting the infinitude of God. We are always petitioning God, that is to say, opening ourselves to the divine generosity, even when we do not ask for anything expressly. And it is significant that the first result of any mystical experience is the acknowledgment of this truth regarding ourselves (needy creatures) and regarding God (from whom all good things come). This sense of the truth becomes most keenly alive in the mystic, and begins to come to the fore during this stage of purification. What was formerly a conviction born of faith now becomes an experience.

Discretion Is Necessary

A certain discretion is necessary here, because dryness in prayer may come from our attachment to the evil we do. In that case, the only thing to do is to collaborate with God in overcoming our evil inclinations. The difficulty is not in our prayer, but in our life. But if the dryness is accompanied by a difficulty in reflecting, and we are seeking God and trying to remain faithful, then we are clearly dealing with a purification, and in this case the "beggar's prayer" may be recommended. We say "may be," because in the first years of prayer we have to do our utmost to apply ourselves to more or less discursive, more or less affective mental prayer, for the reasons we mentioned above. But if a person who really tries to pray finds himself or herself, despite all efforts, for psychological or physiological reasons, up against a wall, it would be good for him or her to try out this remaining quietly before God, cultivating his presence in faith, hope and love. For those who have spent years at meditation and haven't been able to shake off this sense of uselessness, this prayer of waiting presence is the only attitude possible.

Saint John of the Cross lists three signs showing that someone has been placed by the Holy Spirit beyond active mental prayer and has been introduced into mystical prayer, called by him "contemplation."

> The first is the realization that one cannot make discursive meditation nor receive satisfaction from it as before. Dryness is now the outcome of fixing the senses upon subjects which formerly provided satisfaction. . . .
>
> The second sign is an awareness of a disinclination to fix the imagination or sense faculties upon other particular objects, exterior or interior. I am not affirming that the imagination will cease to come and go (even in deep recollection it usually wanders freely), but that the person is disinclined to fix it purposely upon extraneous things.
>
> The third and surest sign is that a person likes to remain alone in loving awareness of God, without particular consideration, in interior peace and quiet and repose and without the acts and exercises (at least discursive, those in which one progresses from point to point) of the intellect, memory and will.[10]

If the three signs appear together it is clear that the person is being introduced into contemplation, but not if only one or two are present. The first sign occurs in people who cannot pray, because of their "dissipation and lack of diligence." But they like to fix their phantasies in other objects. The first and the second signs together afflict people who are subject to psychological depression ("melancholia" in John's vocabulary); there are indeed those who can neither meditate nor find pleasure in anything. When also the third sign is observed, "the loving knowledge and awareness in peace," the person is certainly entering into the marvelous world of contemplation. The presence, more visible, of the first two signs must lead to discern whether the third one is also present.

It must be noticed, nevertheless, that one may enter into this new kind of passive prayer in two different ways. In some cases, it happens in a sudden and total manner: the person who prays can no longer meditate. In other cases it happens gradually: there are days in which one can be active and days in which one cannot do it and is attracted toward peace and silence. In these cases, when it becomes possible, one should occupy himself or herself actively, for example, in reading the scriptures, in talking lovingly to God on the biblical passage, etc., but without making too much effort. We are convinced that people are more often hurt by trying to remain active than by placing themselves simply in God's presence.

Spiritual advisors must not wait until the person who is bound by this spiritual powerlessness shows a strong fidelity to the gospel before recommending her or him to adopt an attitude of loving expectation: first, because, as John of the Cross expressly states, the night of the senses begins soon to darken the prayer life of those who are committed to it with assiduity;[11] second, because this attitude of availability and loving expectation may be useful to people who, because of their temper, find it very difficult to give themselves to a more or less discursive meditation. It is true that in this case other methods may be advisable: Ignatian contemplation, centering prayer, the "Jesus prayer," etc.

But why is it that in both cases of feeling powerless at prayer (the first of psychological origin, the second resulting from spiritual growth) a person has to turn to a simple prayer of waiting, expectant presence? Because, to put it simply, in its very essence prayer consists of opening oneself up to the loving presence of God: making ourselves present to the one who is mysteriously present to us. It would not be out of place to recall the various definitions of prayer that we mentioned above. The two commonest traditional definitions, "lifting up the mind to God," and "conversing with God," entail mutual presence and relationship. The author of *The Cloud of Unknowing* tells us something similar: "Prayer in itself is nothing but a devout reaching out directly to God."[12] St. Teresa of Jesus defines it as "an intimate sharing between friends; it means taking time frequently to be alone with Him who we know loves us,"[13] a "giving our love for His."[14] And speaking to those who alleged they were unable to meditate, she remarks: "I'm not asking you to do anything more than look at Him."[15] All these definitions or descriptions of prayer have one fundamental element in common: in all of them prayer is opening oneself lovingly to the God who is present to us—a mutual presence, a relationship of faith and love. It is not a matter of some sort of abstract consideration on the omnipresence of God by an opening of oneself personally to the divine mystery present in us, in our lives and in the world that surrounds us. Recall that the monastic tradition, from the desert to Bernard, defined the vocation of a monk or a nun as "being always before God like the angels."

How To Behave

I'm going to try to offer a few practical rules of behavior, drawn basically from tradition, on how people ought to behave when, despite their searching for God and striving to remain faithful, they experience nothing in prayer except their own spiritual powerlessness, especially their inability to meditate discursively, and the drying up of their affections.

St. John of the Cross recommends that they do as follows:

> The attitude necessary in the night of sense is to pay no attention to discursive meditation, since this is not the time for it. They should allow the soul to remain in rest and quietude, even though it may seem very obvious to them that they are doing nothing and wasting time, and even though they think this disinclination to think about anything is due to their laxity. Through patience and perseverance in prayer, they will be doing a great deal without activity on their part. All that is required of them here is freedom of soul, that they liberated themselves from the impediment and fatigue of ideas and thoughts and care not about thinking and meditating. They must be content simply with a loving and peaceful attentiveness to God, and live without the concern, without the effort, and without the desire to taste or feel Him. All these desires disquiet the soul and distract it. . . . [16]

We need a loving and peaceful attentiveness to God, without forcing ourselves to meditate or getting upset because we don't experience God's action in us. St. John of the Cross wrote this between 1582 and 1585.

About ten years earlier, Fr. Baltasar Alvarez had said practically the same thing as he was describing the attitude needed in prayer by those who have left discursive meditation (and every form of prayer in which human activity predominates) behind them:

> They should stand reverently in the presence of God
> . . . opening their heart and their needs to Him, without

talking much, or even without talking at all. Because
God understand this from the mere fact that the needy
one presents him or herself before Him. Just as the poor
who merely stand there before us have no need to
speak, because their need speaks for itself, so (those
who pray thus) wait for the mercy of God with entire
resignation to the divine will, both as to the amount and
the manner in which He may choose to give them, regarding themselves as being unworthy of his glance and
his favors.[17]

Father Alvarez had, then, already recommended that
we do the same thing that St. John of the Cross later ad-
vised: to remain open, with love and reverence, to the presence of God, without saying much or anything, and leave it
to God to care for the kind, time and manner of prayer we
are to have in the future. We must look for God alone and
therefore be content to stand in God's presence.

St. Teresa, although she was addressing persons who
were afraid of entering the ways of mental prayer (judging
it not to be meant for them), nevertheless pointed toward
some broader horizons when she recommended the following to those who were unable to meditate:

I'm not asking you now that you think about Him or that
you draw out a lot of concepts or make long and subtle
reflections with your intellect. I'm not asking you to do
anything more than look at Him. . . . Well, now daughters, your Spouse never takes His eyes off you.[18]

It is, then, a matter of looking with love on one who looks
on us with love.

And so we have the witness of three masters, two of
them publicly recognized by the church as doctors of spiritual teaching.

Be Still and Know That I Am God

Reading through these paragraphs from some of the classics of Catholic spirituality, some readers may have felt the words of the psalmist stir in their memory: "Be still and know that I am God." We need (God help us!) to remember these words, for there is nothing harder than being and keeping quiet very long. Everything seems to be pushing us into movement when we most want to be quiet: memories, preoccupations, what we are going to do, dates we must keep . . . Yet the Spirit insists: "Be still and know that I am God." God had asked something similar of Israel through the prophet Isaiah. God's people were putting their trust in human means and wanted to obtain their own salvation in a hurry: "Upon horses we will flee . . . upon swift steeds we will ride." But the Holy One of Israel kept repeating:

> By waiting and by calm you shall be saved,
> in quiet and in trust your strength lies (Is 30:15).

In reality, even though waiting becomes heavy for us in proportion to the good we are hoping for and the intensity of our desires, waiting is nonetheless something very human, because every human being is a project whose complete realization is always beyond; our whole existence is at once a hoping and a waiting. Waiting, it should be noted, is simply the temporal dimension of hoping. The child hoped to become an adult, and waits for this with toys or books in hand. Young people hope to get a job, to get married and have children, and they wait. A lover hopes and waits for a call from the beloved. Someone who has applied for a job hopes and waits for an answer. We hope to have a happy old age and a peaceful death. We hope, always, and we wait. In prayer we hope that the Spirit will begin to immerse us in the mystery of God, and we wait while we are being prepared for it. In reality, we are waiting for ourselves, because God is always prompt, while we need time in order to be ourselves.

But in fact, this hoping and waiting that will find its realization in an encounter with God in the deepest depths of ourselves is a homage to the divine sovereignty and transcendence. Believing is translated immediately into hoping: we submit ourselves to God, hoping for God's final revelation. In the words of Jesus and in the Christian scriptures, believing and hoping tend to blend. For neither the present nor the past can exhaust the divine mystery. The future, like an unfinished sentence, best reflects the infiniteness of God. Thus it is that the believer goes through his or her whole spiritual itinerary, invaded by wonder (God always seems to be "improvised") and awaiting new surprises. "By waiting and by calm," we acknowledge that God is God, and we do not try to prevent God from being God by reducing God's ways to our ways.

A Most General Way

In the past, we used to learn the methods of prayer carefully and we strove to follow them faithfully, although it was always added that we must above all follow the movements of the Spirit. Today we tend to go to the opposite extreme: an excess of spontaneity.

Basing our remarks essentially on what we have just read from Teresa, John and Fr. Alvarez, and adding one important plus (scripture reading, because of our easy access to modern versions of the Bible), we can deduce a very general method for prayer during this phase of waiting, which can be a rather long one. Let us describe its various phases.

1. All prayer obviously begins with opening ourselves to the presence of God and trying to remain in peace before the divine mystery. Since prayer is above all mutual presence, it should be clear that we have to begin by opening our consciousness and our heart to this presence. All of the wit-

nesses of the Spirit have recommended this as the first step in personal prayer. We should gather up the faculties of our psyche and take a deep breath of the infinite love that surrounds us.

2. Once we have made this first contact with God and have pacified our wandering faculties to the best of our ability, we may proceed to a slow and attentive reading of a scripture passage. This is what St. Francis Borgia counseled St. Teresa to do: "that I should always begin prayer with an event from the Passion."[19] For us, it might be the gospel or the first reading from the liturgy of the day, which would have the added benefit of putting us in tune with the spirit of the Church.

In ascetical or active prayer, the scripture passage may have served us as a text for reflection and may have suggested the sort of response we should make to God. Here, however, it is a matter of entering, by means of this slow reading, into an ambiance of faith and love. But it should be noted that the Lord of the scriptures may already have moved us in another way, for example, by making some biblical antiphon from the liturgy of the hours resonate in our heart. We should follow the movements of the Spirit.

Why should we ordinarily begin with the slow reading of a biblical text? For several reasons. First and foremost because, as we know, personal prayer is a response to the God who has spoken to us in the scriptures, and definitively in Christ. We have to begin by listening, by letting ourselves be touched and molded by the word of God. Second, because the reading will often provide us with some attribute of God or some trait or title of Christ Jesus on which we can center our attention: Jesus who proclaims the forgiveness of sins, Jesus who heals, Jesus who gives sight to the blind. Or else it may suggest an attitude that suits us: that of the blind man asking for sight, that of the woman who wept at his feet, that of Mary at the foot of the cross or that of Magdalene announcing the resurrection.

3. After finishing the reading, we may close the book

and concentrate more directly on the presence of God, in a sort of general gaze. Now and then we may utter some invocation. An excellent one might be the traditional prayer of the eastern church: "Lord Jesus Christ, Son of the living God, have mercy on me, a sinner." Or we might simply repeat the name of God or of Jesus, or, if we prefer, some petition taken from the reading, for example, "Lord, that I may see."

But note that this is not a matter of tiring ourselves out by repeating words, which might be an unconscious attempt to turn back to "making our own prayer." The prayer we're talking about doesn't consist of speaking much or little, but of letting God be God and of placing ourselves in the presence of the divine mystery in an attitude of service or hopeful waiting, and always love. These invocations should not be repeated forcibly or even, as a general rule, frequently. They may come to us from time to time, to help us concentrate our loving gaze on God.

4. Even our body position can be a prayer: holding our palms open on our lap, like someone begging for an alms, for example. Sometimes we may sit on our haunches like the servants of antiquity, or even prostrate ourselves with our face to the ground, when we are overcome at the thought of our lowliness. But our bodily attitude should come as the result of our inner state, not of some premeditated plan. Ordinarily we spend the greater part of our prayer seated comfortably on a cushion or in our chair, in order to avoid being distracted by our body. India knows a great deal about the importance of the body for contemplation.

5. As much as possible, we should remain in this simple and loving attention to the infinite God for the whole time we have set for prayer. Fidelity to this point is most important. We can't withdraw from prayer simply because we don't seem to be getting anything out of it (which might mean that we're looking for ourselves, rather than God), or because we are suffering during prayer. Fidelity is often the only prayer we can offer. But we have to have at least this.

If we get distracted, we should calmly bring ourselves back to God's presence. Friends can get distracted during conversation without necessarily offending one another. Distractions do not interrupt prayer when they are involuntary. As often as we catch ourselves being distracted, we should just as often turn our eyes back to gaze on God.

6. We have done all that we can by placing ourselves before God like the poor people we are—but like poor people who are in love. It will be seen that all the rest—invocations, body positions, etc.—are possible, but not necessary, means. Sometimes even the initial scripture reading may be omitted when we feel already moved to place ourselves in God's presence.

This very general method is useful during this time of dryness that lies beyond discursive meditation and affective prayer. But it turns out to be only method (or, rather, attitude) possible when one is already in the prayer of quiet, or of simple or ecstatic union, because in these phases one is not always in the highest level attained thus far. Passive prayer can come or not come. What does one do in the meantime? One simply places oneself in God's presence. The prayer of presence will occasionally be changed into an explosion of peace and joy or into the experience of being possessed and dominated by grace, etc. In that case, God has responded to our hopeful waiting, letting us feel the prayer that God's own Spirit is making within us. But at other times we may be left in waiting, because nobody can force God's Spirit.

7

Approaching Mystical Experience

One day the door opens. A person has spent a greater or lesser number of years (the Spirit has no calendar) standing outside humbly, in hope, like a poor beggar, before a closed door. Suddenly the door is opened and the beggar (Lazarus, Elizabeth or whoever) is invited to enter the foyer, which is already lit from a distance by the glory that filters through from the inmost room. Little by little the beggar will be invited to come further inside, room after room, until he or she reaches the central chamber where God is at the festal banquet. The author of these lines is well aware that he is using the old, delightful image of a house or castle with many rooms. In sober fact, as Teresa clearly saw, the metaphor is really about entering the depths of ourselves until, transcending ourselves, we meet the Creator and Redeemer God.

A Scholarly Discussion

Almost a century ago, when studies in spiritual theology were experiencing a rebirth in Europe, especially in France and Spain, a lively debate arose between the theologians of different schools on the question of whether mystical experience is the normal flowering of everyone's spiritual life or whether, on the contrary, it is an extraordinary grace to which only a special few are called. In fact, the discussion occasionally became quite heated. Naturally, both groups cited the classics, especially St. John of the Cross and St. Teresa of Jesus, to bolster their opinion.

The members of the first group,[1] heirs to the common theological vision of the eighteenth and nineteenth centuries, defended the existence of two separate ways to reach the fulness of Christian life. One, the King's Highway of Rodríguez, was for the majority of Christians. It consisted of ascetical progress due to human efforts, sustained by the grace of God. Simply by traveling this highway one could come to a union with God's will and, by that very fact, holiness. These people, the majority of Christians (or so Rodríguez said), spend their whole lives experiencing only their own activities and efforts, praying vocally, meditating, consciously summoning up their own affections—all under the grace of God. Others, in contrast, a small band of chosen ones, walk on unmarked paths that are "lofty and perilous," because all sorts of illusions lurk in the surrounding bushes. These paths run along crooked lines, marked by extraordinary experiences (visions, words, wounds of love and even, perhaps, revelations and prophecies). If the Spirit of God should choose to lead us along these fearful ways, we must (so they said) submit, but such experiences could not be desired and, should they be granted one, one would have to accept them with discretion and with some trepidation. There were two distinct ways: the ascetical way, tried and true and with no surprises, on the one hand, and the mystical way, uncharted and beset with surprises and dangers, on the other.

The opposite group of theologians,[2] taking their starting point from the commonly held theology of the gifts of the Holy Spirit, defended the position that there is but one "way" to reach Christian maturity, and this way is made up of a number of one-day journeys that are mainly ascetical (i.e., where we *experience* our growth as the result of our fidelity and effort, although we firmly *believe* that it is radically the result of grace), and of other, advanced journeys that are mystical, in which we feel that we are invaded, moved, taken and left by someone whom we cannot control. During these latter journeys, prayer tends to be transformed into a surprise, because we can't foresee what the Spirit is going to do or cease doing with us. Is she going to flood us with her presence and light, or is she going to leave us sitting on the ground emptyhanded?

Universal Call

This second opinion is nowadays by far the commoner one, although today, in the light of further theological findings and presuppositions, the question may be stated in different ways. Today it is most commonly held that if we remain faithful to prayer, it will tend to flower forth in a succession of joyful or sorrowful experiences over which we have no control either to induce them or ward them off, and during which we sense the active presence of the living God. Those who undergo or suffer (that is the ancient definition of mysticism: suffering the divine) these experiences, attribute them to the Holy Spirit. Why? Not mainly because they cannot bring them on or even, in some cases, prevent them from happening. Today we know that many of our experiences are not limited to the sphere of our conscious or voluntary ego. There are things that well up from the depths of our psyche (dreams, visions or words, powerful feelings) without the involvement of our consciousness or will. Those who undergo the experiences we call mystical attribute them to the Holy Spirit because they are accompanied by a sense of certainty of the presence and action of God within us and are only meaningful if interpreted in this way. The decisive point, then, is not verifying whether at least some of these experiences come from the deep regions of our psyche, beyond consciousness (which we can't know, anyway), but, rather, establishing the fact that a human subject perceives the presence and action of the

divine Spirit and experiences that he or she is being gradually possessed by God. Such are the experiences of union.
Those who listen to the testimony of a mystic do not acquire
the full certainty that the mystic has during these moments,
but they can discern the active presence of God through the
effects that they see in the mystics themselves: displaying
uncommon acts of love for God and their neighbor, overcoming traumas, pardoning offenses, revealing truths that are
burdensome to themselves. Only those who begin with the
presupposition (or prejudice) that God does not act as
Spirit, moving and directing our spirit, will feel forced to
deny this active presence of God in the mystic.

The writer of these lines is firmly convinced that every
intense life of prayer—provided no impediments are placed
in its way—tends to issue in mystical experience. This is because the Holy Spirit dwells with her gifts in the "hearts"
of all believers. When faith takes possession of us, then
there is a necessary flowering of what theology, inspired
by Isaiah 11:2-3, has come to call "the gifts of the Holy
Spirit"—wisdom, understanding, counsel, etc.—interpret-
ing them (beyond the force of the original text) to mean an
experiential knowledge of God, or, rather, an enlighten-
ment concerning God and of creatures of God. Hope appears
as an extraordinary force, and love appears as a childlike
relationship that animates everything. Only the Spirit
knows the spirituality of God, and wherever the Spirit is
firmly lodged, she never fails to communicate that spirituality religiously.

But we need to spell out more precisely what is meant
by mystical experience. In every religious experience, the
God who is implicit in every act of knowing and loving, as
the reality that gives meaning to all things, is in some way
made explicit. That is to say, the believer becomes conscious of this presence. But once the first theophany or God-
awareness takes place in faith, the believer can repeat it
voluntarily by turning to God in prayer or in silent contemplation. This is ordinary religious experience. Mystical ex-

perience is a perception of this mysterious presence with such force that its received and unbidden character is evident to the one who has it. Those who have this theophany experience it as a sheer grace that surprises them with new insights, enriches them with powerful experiences of love, and incredibly strengthens them. According to the testimony of the mystics themselves, mystical experience essentially boils down to one thing: a perception of the presence and activity of God in us, opening us to the divine mystery. The successive degrees of this experience are varying degrees of intensity in perceiving this active presence that overtakes us.

Christian Tradition on Mysticism

Christian theology began very early on to be concerned with contemplative phenomena. There were already a few scripture texts that laid the ground for this. The very word *ecstasy* (extasis), which occurred frequently enough in the Greek translation of the Hebrew Bible, appears three times in the Acts of the Apostles in the context of visions: twice with reference to Peter (10:10 and 11:5) and once with reference to Paul (22:17). Paul, referring to himself in the third person, says that he was caught up to the third heaven, where he heard ineffable words (2 Cor 12:2ff). This did not escape the attention of the fathers. Naturally, too, we cannot forget the "visions" of the Apocalypse, which served as a cultural model for the first visionaries of the Middle Ages. Something similar had been noticed among the first masters of Christian spirituality. Anthony, the father of anchorites, once went into ecstasy and began to weaken under the weight of certain prophetic insights he received.[3] The fathers and mothers of the desert, who were committed to a life of prayer and manual labor, seem to have had certain intense experiences frequently.

On these data, and on their own personal life-experiences, the fathers focused their attention. There is, they tell us, a knowledge (*gnosis* or *theoria*) of God that is proper of the "perfect" and superior to simple knowledge derived from accepting the truths of faith (Clement of Alexandria, d. 215). This knowledge is a gift of God and not the fruit of our activity, added Origen (d. 254),[4] whose teaching was frequently repeated by John Cassian (d. 435).[5] One arrives at this knowledge by a three-stage process, which Gregory of Nyssa (d. 394) calls "action" (ascetical or service-oriented), "in the cloud" (assiduous meditation) and "in the dark" (characterized by a sense of the divine presence).[6] This obsure vision of God, says Gregory, is founded on the indwelling of the triune God in us, and entails the union of our spirit with the transcendent God. The obscure or unfinished aspect of contemplative experience was developed through the "dark" strain of mysticism that ran through the Middle Ages to St. John of the Cross. In it we are repeatedly told that we do not see God *in se*, but rather, as Pseudo-Dionysius would say, "the place of God," that is, some of God's attributes.[7] In contrast, the strain of "light" mysticism (running from Origen to Pseudo Macarius and Maximus the Confessor) stresses the ocean of light that overwhelms the contemplative.

Mystical experience is not something purely intellectual, but involves both intelligence and love. Both elements are fused in it: the mystic is united to God in love, and in understanding without understanding. Gregory of Nyssa, who was both a theologian and a mystic, was acquainted with the various phenomena of ecstasy, sober inebriation, watchful sleep and a sense of spiritual dizziness. Little by little, *ecstasy*, whereby the soul leaves everything visible behind it (Origen, Gregory of Nyssa) or even transcends its own (Pseudo-Dionysius), becomes the common term used to designate every contemplative experience. John Cassian, in contrast, speaks of a "prayer of fire,"[8] and identifies ectasis with a particular phenomenon.[9]

While the western spiritual writers of the twelfth century generally stress the gratuitous and passive character of mystical experience (God is the one, says Bernard, who—like the lover in the Song of Songs—lifts us up to "the kiss of his mouth")[10] and insist on the fusion of love and understanding, the Rhineland mystics of the fourteenth century (Eckhardt, Tauler and Suso) remind us of the deepest foundation of mystical experience. God is Being and creatures are nothing. God dwells in the very depth of the soul, grounding and giving it being. Mystical experience is, then, a re-encounter with the being that is the source of being; it is an experience that takes place in the depths or the point of the soul. St. John of the Cross (sixteenth century) brings together this twofold—monastic and speculative—medieval tradition.

Mystics and Visionaries

It is interesting to note how, throughout ancient tradition, true mystical experience takes place beyond the imagination, in the understanding or the will or, more radically, in the depth of our being. It is a purely spiritual experience. In our preceding explanation of mysticism, no reference was made to the numerous visions with images or to the multiple words (sometimes rather long speeches) which some mystics seem to see and hear. The reason is now clear: they do not belong to the very core of mystical experience. They are secondary and accidental phenomena. They can be found or not found in mystics, whereas they appear to be the sole or predominant phenomena in people who do not seem to echo the traits of real mystical experience as described by the Christian tradition.

When the fathers speak of "vision" in connection with mystical experience, they are referring to a vision of the understanding, or a purely spiritual vision. Augustine classifies visions into intellectual, imaginative and corporeal. Perhaps they might be reduced to two—vision by the understanding and by the imagination. What is the nature of the images that accompany mystical experience? We believe that St. Bernard hit upon the answer with his explanation: "A vision of God suddenly shines *into the mind* with the swiftness of a lightning-flash. Immediately, but whence I do not know, images of earthly things fill the imagination, either as an aid to understand or to temper the intensity of the divine light. . . . My opinion is that they are formed in our imaginations by the inspirations of the holy angels, just as on the other hand there is no doubt that evil suggestions of an opposite nature are forced upon us by the bad angels."[11] Respectfully leaving the matter of the holy angels aside, and not even thinking of the bad ones, we might prefer to speak in terms of the light and dark sides of our own psyche.

This leads us to focus on a distinction which has heretofore received little or no attention: the one that differentiates a mystic from a visionary. Let us go back to the definition of mystical experience that we have just offered: a gradually overpowering experience in which a human being feels himself or herself to be in the presence of the God of mystery, possessed more or less powerfully by God's grace and united to God. This presence and unitive action is variously translated into experiences of love and of light for the understanding. Toward the end of the mystic journey, the light tends to take the form of certain visions of the divine attributes, in which the increasing penetration of the truth is accompanied by a strong sense of the divine presence. The mystic feels that he or she is in the presence of the divine goodness or is, so to speak, in the midst of God, that is, among the Father, the Son and the life-giving Spirit of God. But for most mystics, the greater part of their way is characterized by a light which makes all their religious symbols burst and blossom into meaning, and not by way of any objects seen. The mystic begins to see everything in an all-renewing, morning light, without having visions. As for "hearing," throughout their journey all mystics feel periodically addressed by God, invited by God to love, or reproached by God for their failings. Sometimes these "addresses" are inserted into the very weft and woof of prayer. At other times, in contrast, the Christian feels suddenly and powerfully challenged or exhorted, so that these "words" retain some of their original power, instilling in him or her a desire and longing for greater purity and love, together with a lively sense of his or her own frailty and misery.

But there are other believers in whom this essential mystical experience (the awareness of the divine presence and action) makes their whole psyche resonate in a special way, so that it bursts forth in manifold and varied phenomena of visions and words. The most varied and beautiful images (or the most monstrous ones, in cases of demoniacal experiences) follow upon one another in rapid succession. Words, even whole discourses, are heard. In this case, the mystic is at once a mystic and a visionary. These are usually people with a lively and creative imagination, and of an active and intense psychological makeup, which in turn tends to be expressed inwardly in what they see and/or hear. Through these images and words, the society in which they live is reflected, because the prevailing images they see are those to which they are accustomed, and the words they hear often embody the accepted theology of the day, or else the theology which their spiritual director or some favorite spiritual author has been suggesting to them. In other cases, the mystic's own acute intelligence may be set in motion and provide us with some theological insights properly so-called. Note that we are speaking of mystics who are at the same time visionaries. The images they see are merely the outward dressing in which their psyche clothes an experience of the divine presence and action that take place at a much deeper level of their being. It is not, then, a matter of images which the psyche in its ordinary state can reconstruct at will. Rather, these images present themselves with a unique vividness and beauty that leave a profound impression. They greatly enliven the love and strengthen the will of those who experience them. In these mystic-visionaries, ecstasy tends to be much more frequent during the time they are going through the ecstatic union. As is well known, ecstasy is at one and the same time the result of the power of the mystic's experience, on the one hand, and, on the other, of the weakness of a psyche that is easily carried away by this experience, so as to lose contact with the outer world.

These lively and active imaginations, with a tendency to live in an inner world populated by images and words, are often found in persons who give every appearance of suffering or of having suffered certain psychic imbalances. Sometimes they occur in persons who are suffering or have suffered some trauma, such as the powerful onset of affectivity, a great inclination to love that had been obstructed by external circumstances (e.g., in the case of medieval nuns who were taken away from their parents at the age of ten or twelve), the early loss or absence of a father or mother, etc. We say "often" and "sometimes," but not "necessarily," because there are mystic-visionaries who seem to enjoy the sturdiest physical and mental health. But when a mystic-visionary in fact bears the burden of a trauma or seems to suffer from some imbalance, his or her mystical experience is initially more painful, yet is gradually healed through the therapeutic power of grace.

Moreover, individuals can be visionaries without really being mystics. This is the case when all their experiences boil down to a number of visions and words, while neither their spiritual directors nor those who read their written testimonies can detect in them any note of an experience of the loving presence and action of God. Visionaries of this sort speak only of what they see—and they see a great deal. But they speak a great deal less about what they feel, and even from the little that they do say about this, one can't seem to detect the kind of mystical experience which is disclosed in real mystical experience. These non-mystical visionaries are people who are suffering from some affective imbalance or from some other psychic disorder, and hence take refuge in this sort of intense psychic life.

A Few Examples

Perhaps the reader would appreciate our giving a few examples of the three types we have just distinguished. Of the third type (visionaries who are not mystics), it is practically impossible to offer any examples, because the memory of such persons usually ends with their death. Not only that, but their inner creativity often dries up long before they die. In the course of their work, all long-experienced spiritual directors will have run across men and women of this sort.

Some examples of pure mystics (those who have had few or practically no imaginative visions, discourses or bodily phenomena) are Ignatius Loyola, John of the Cross, Jane Frances de Chantal, Marie of the Incarnation, Elizabeth Ann Seton, Elizabeth of the Trinity and Edith Stein. Let us dwell for a moment on the first two. Ignatius had some very high mystical experiences; those of Manresa and Rome are well known. In his final years he was in a constant contemplative attitude, typical of the "Seventh Mansion." Nevertheless, he found it hard to "hear" and above all "see" with his imagination. The comparison he uses to convey the sense of a vision of the Trinity (a musical chord) reveals the non-fanciful turn of mind of a former Basque soldier. No one can deny the exalted mystical experience that shines through the pages of John of the Cross; yet no visions of the fantasy are attributed to him. Certainly, the "mystical doctor" par excellence has left us no record of them in his autobiography, in his diary or in his letters to his confessor. But it is significant that whereas a truly personal tone peeps through when he speaks of love-wounds and intellectual visions, he seems to echo his studies and reflections when he deals with corporeal and imaginative visions, and when he deals with successive locutions ("heard" speeches), he clearly manifests his surprise at what he discovered in others. In American spirituality, Elizabeth Ann Seton had some very keen experiences of the fatherly love of God and the presence of Christ, yet it is hard to find in her writings any echo of that different sort of experience that abounds in the visionary. Thomas Merton, even as a student, enjoyed at least the prayer of quiet. We know this from one of his sporadic admissions. Unfortunately, however, he was very reserved on what went on between him and God, and we cannot follow his development very closely. But he was certainly not a visionary. Turning our attention to one of the classics, Teresa of Jesus (perhaps the reader has been wondering where we would classify her), we would have to say that she was above all a great mystic, although these secondary phenomena we have been referring to seem to have occurred rather frequently in her experience. Even so, such images and words were not predominant in Teresa's religious experience.[12]

The interior life of mystics who were also visionaries is more immediately perceptible, even by the uninitiated reader, because the experiences which they describe are easier to narrate and to understand. In this group are Elizabeth of Schoenau, Gertrude and Mechtild of Hackeborn, Hadewijch, Jeanne Chézard de Matel, Margaret Mary Alacoque and the Jesuit Bernardo Hoyos. Gertrude (starting from her total commitment to God when she was twenty years old) and Mechtild seem to have encountered the Lord in every corner of the dormitory and choir of their monastery. The experience of spousal love with God, developed by the Flemish mystic Hadewijch, is really intense and admirable. This is what stands out in her own experience and in the teaching she wanted to inculcate. Nevertheless, she also had several imaginative visions and heard a number of words during them. Mère de Matel saw and heard the Lord continually. Moreover, she saw before her eyes the most beautiful objects which kept changing, so to speak, magically, in order to express symbolically certain truths concerning the saints. The less numerous visions of Margaret Mary have something of a baroque splendor about them.

The Goal of the Life of Prayer

We believe that the reader will now have a clearer idea of the goal of an intense life of prayer. When Teresa of Jesus tells us that it is an excellent thing to desire to enter even the final mansion of the Interior Castle and that God will not close the door on those who seek to do so,[13] she is speaking of nothing more than that encounter with the Lord who is lovingly present, that total union of our faculties and even of our very being with God, which constitutes the mystical journey. And when we speak of union, we are not referring to the simple union of our will with the will of God, but to the invasion of our faculties and of our very being, in an experiential way, by grace. But neither Teresa of Jesus nor the other witnesses who have spoken of the one spiritual way for all have proposed, as the goal of our desires, those other wonderful phenomena (situated more on the borderline between the psychic and the spiritual) that have made the life of visionary mystics so surprising.

8

The Higher Degrees of Prayer

We are going to try to describe the successive prayer that is commonly called "mystical." We have seen how the fathers, above all Gregory of Nyssa, described various phenomena observed in prayer. In contrast, St. Augustine, breaking his customary reserve to speak of his own experience in a few isolated texts, refers to various aspects of what we now call mystical experience.[1] In the light of these texts, a new meaning came to be attached to a number of terms that Augustine often used to describe any type of religious experience, and not just mystical experience: peace, quiet, rejoicing, leaving the visible behind and entering into the depths of oneself. But none of the fathers, or even the spiritual writers of the middle ages up to the twelfth century, attempt to give us a description of the various stages through which mystics may pass, once they have reached this third phase of which we have been speaking. Those who do speak of the various stages of contemplation refer to religious experience in general and describe these stages in terms of the objects contemplated in them, rather than in terms of the transformation they mark in the subjects.

It is in eastern Christianity, especially in Syria, that the attention of the mystics seem to have been first attracted to the succession of various degrees of contemplation. Isaac of Nineveh (second half of the seventh century) describes first what he calls *delight during prayer*, then *contemplation* or *vision in prayer*, without images, and finally *non-prayer*, or a state of passivity, stillness and wonder.[2] Isaac states very clearly three different stages and even affirms that the second one, *contemplation*, has various degrees.

In western Europe, the twelfth century brought the discovery of the individual, especially in the area of personal feelings and experiences.[3] Bernard expressly refers to the "book of our experience"[4] and when speaking of contemplation frequently appeals to the experience of his listeners.[5] But here again we find that the discussion stops short at contemplation, without distinguishing any further degrees in it. St. Bernard speaks of the three degrees of the spiritual way: kissing Christ's feet (that is, conversion), kissing Christ's hands (that is, ascetical progress) and kissing Christ's mouth (that is, contemplation).[6] The various phases of contemplative experience are condensed into the one biblical metaphor of "the kiss of his mouth."

Nevertheless, even then, there were a few attempts at distinguishing successive phases in contemplative experience. In commentaries on the Song of Songs, mention is made both of the kiss which the spouse received and of her subsequent falling asleep. The Scottish-born Richard of St. Victor (d. 1173) sketched out a first description of the four degrees of overpowering (or, as he calls it, "violent") love: love that wounds one with the feeling of presence, love which binds memory and thought, exclusive love which takes us out of ourselves and unites our will to God's, and the love of God according to God which issues in total commitment and passivity.[7]

With the great women mystics of the middle ages, beginning with Elizabeth of Schonau, and above all, from the thirteenth century on, we begin to find autobiographical accounts of mystical experiences. Gertrude of Helfta, Mechtild of Hackeborn and Hadewijch have left us a narrative of their visions. Personal experience shines through in yet other writings, for example those of Mechtild of Magdeburg. They mark an intense flowering of autobiographical literature, in which the language and terminology of mystical experience was gradually honed to a certain precision. While Gertrude's language, for example, is still rather generic, the effects of her "revelations" are now and then disclosed: strong desires, depression, melting of the heart, feeling filled abundantly with the Holy Spirit.[8] In one passage where she expressly cites Bernard, Gertrude speaks of a "vision without images."[9] The description of mystical states becomes even more plastic in the writings of the Flemish poet and mystic Hadewijch: "God embraced me in my interior senses and took me away in spirit"; "My senses were drawn inward with a great tempestuous clamor"; "I experienced desires and an exceedingly strong longing"; "My heart and my veins and all my limbs trembled and quivered."[10]

But what these women described (although as no one before them had done) were happenings, not stages. It remained for the men of the age to try their hand at describing the itinerary of contemplation. John Ruusbroec, a mystic and theologian (the combination has always produced good results), in one of his first treatises, "The Spiritual Spousals," describes and reflects on the spiritual itinerary from what he calls the active life (the life of beginners) up to perfect union, which he calls contemplative life. It should be noted, however, that the intermediate or, as he calls it, the interior life is in turn made up of three successive comings of Christ: the first is characterized first by consolations and then by desolation; the second is compared to a fountain with three great jets of grace which invade the three faculties; the third is compared with the wellspring which feeds the fountain and consists of divine touches during which the soul is perfectly passive. With the second and third of these "comings of Christ" the soul enters more and more deeply into mystical experience. The "contemplative life" described in Book Three is full mystical union: "being God with God without intermediaries," "contemplating God with God without intermediaries," and contemplatives in this sense "are transformed and become one with the very light by which they see and which they see."[11]

But it remained again for a great woman of the sixteenth century, Teresa of Jesus, to give us a more precise and detailed description of the way of contemplation, which she based essentially on her own experience, although she found help in clarifying her thought from a few well-read treatises by the Franciscan writers Francisco de Osuna (d. 1540) and Bernardo de Laredo (d. 1540). In Teresa, the psychological aspect of mystical experience (which is as essential for understanding of mystical experience as theology is) reaches an almost definitive clarification. A good number of men and women mystics after her time refer to the same stages as she does, and her description has become part of the common heritage of various schools of spirituality in the Christian west. We are fundamentally going to follow Teresa's categories in order to explain the various degrees of mystical experience.

Drawn into Oneself

The first experience that people have when their prayer begins to well up spontaneously from the depths, beyond the control of their will, is what has come to be called the prayer of recollection. Teresa of Jesus, in her account to Fr. Rodrigo Alvarez, says that this is "the first prayer I felt that was in my opinion supernatural," that is (and Teresa goes on to explain what she means here by supernatural), the kind of prayer "which cannot be acquired by industry or diligence, however much one strives."[12] In the Fourth Mansion, where she inserts a digression on the prayer of recollection, speaking of the later prayer of quiet, she tells us: "In the case of this recollection, it doesn't come when we want it, but when God wants to grant us the favor."[13] Whatever our theological categories might be, there is no confusing the sort of recollection or interiorization that is normal for us at a certain stage in our lives, with these states of profound and gentle recollection that come and go without our being able to bid or stop them, and which the witnesses of the Spirit experience as a grace of God.

What does this experience consist of? For those who receive it, it consists of their feeling drawn gently inward, immersed in an atmosphere of reverence and love. They experience it as something they receive, not only because they do not have to make any effort to achieve it, but also because this atmosphere seems to form around the core of a rather lively sentiment of the divine presence. But it appears essentially as a firm attention to God present within them. They spontaneously close their eyes in order to concentrate on what is occurring within them. There are no great, flashing experiences, but only a greater or lesser sweetness and a tender, loving gaze. Grace acts on their understanding, attracting, so to speak, the curiosity of their creative imagination, although the latter may come and go as it wills. Their psyche is still active; memory and imagination move freely. Hence it is possible to consider one or another aspect of the mystery of God or of Christ, although without much reflection or effort. Their intuitive gaze prevails, sustained by their attention to the Presence.[14] Hence, the interior activity of those who experience this prayer of recollection is not notably distinct from the prayer of simple regard while waiting, which we recommended in the previous chapter. The difference is that before it was a matter of waiting, and no particular response met the soul's gaze. Here, on the contrary, there is a sense of a firm attraction to God, who is felt as being very near.

It is a somewhat tenuous experience, above all if it is compared to the ones that are to follow. Hence, its characteristics do not remain vividly impressed on the memory. It comes suddenly, but the first hints of it, in the form of interior movements or touches, may come before one enters into prayer, even in the midst of absorbing work. These touches or movements are perceived as calls to withdraw. God is preparing us for a mutual encounter in solitude. Note also that later on, when one has already gone more deeply inward, these touches or movements will be repeated before the prayer of quiet or that of union. At other times this recollection will suddenly appear after a painful time during which one has been struggling in vain to concentrate. Or else it will overtake one at the beginning of prayer, without one's having experienced anything in advance. Suddenly one's attention is gently drawn inward and one begins to become vaguely aware of the Presence.

Here, the believer meets the Presence, begins to become experientially aware of (not just accepting in faith) God's loving company. If we were to compare this initial experience with what happens in human relationships, we would say that this experience of recollection is somewhat like the first sympathetic attraction we feel for someone who is going to become our close friend or spouse. Even when that person is surrounded by others, he or she begins to stand out, to manifest himself or herself to us, and our attention feels drawn to what he or she does or says. He or she appears to us as a person, as someone present to us, and our personality turns toward him or her.

The Prayer of Quiet

The first form of prayer that powerfully invades us is called the prayer of quiet, because one of its most characteristic traits is a very strong inner peace. Sometimes it comes suddenly, perhaps after a long spell during which we have been trying in vain to concentrate and calm ourselves. In such cases it strikes like the sudden opening of a sluice-gate, carrying us off in an unexpected wave. At other times it comes very gradually, and the person praying can sense its coming. A very apt comparison is the one St. Teresa gives us when she speaks of a trough that is near a fountain and begins to be filled with water from within until it rises and overflows.[15] This is exactly the impression this prayer has on those who experience it. Something has opened up the depth of their spirit, and it rises and rises, permeating and filling all the faculties of the soul and even the body. At one stroke, this experience takes away all their weariness. We call it a "very strong peace," because it is not like the normal state of rest or relaxation. It is a force which at once powerfully dominates and pacifies its recipient. It may even induce a deep sleep or lethargy of the faculties of the soul. Should others happen to pass by at the time, they might think that the person in this state was fast asleep (in ecstasy). They would be mistaken.

But peace is but one trait of this experience. The soul feels the nearness of God and is filled with joy, sometimes bursting into acts of love or praise or gratitude. We say "bursting," because the sentiments well up powerfully in great rushes and firebursts from within, although more commonly there is an attempt to curtail these acts, and discursive reason is suspended. There can be various degrees of intensity in the course of one and the same experience, above all when it is prolonged. Sometimes the sense of presence and the surge of affections predominate, while at other times the sentiments fade away and the soul is left in a more or less strong state of peace. For the experience can last a whole hour or even longer, if one continues in prayer.

The body feels the muscles relax and even, in stronger experience, fall into lethargy. The respiration can become deep and rhythmic, as in sleep. And yet, the person is alert within. The senses are awake, although it takes an effort to open the eyes and an even greater effort to come out from inside in order to respond to anyone else. Noises can be heard and this may be a cause of distraction. But the fact that the hearing remains intact and may even seem to be keener than usual as a connector with the outside world can be very useful, especially when the experience occurs or continues during the liturgy, because this allows the one experiencing it to unite himself or herself, if not in words, then in affections, with the unfolding of the liturgy.

Although the will is submerged in this great, joyful quiet and the understanding's attention is drawn to the divine Presence, memory and imagination can cause distractions. However, these distractions do not disturb the soul's quiet or its joy in God's presence. The influence of this form of prayer on both the psyche and the body is so strong that it lasts in some way for hours afterward. There is a tendency to enter anew within the self, even when one is in the midst of a conversation or is being bombarded by the signs and sounds of a television set. It often happens that when the person, even after three or four hours, is once again recollected in solitude, the effects are reproduced, almost as if the grace were being repeated. There remains at least a deep sense of gratitude toward the Lord.

This does not mean that those who receive this grace of prayer should go looking for it. Although they should receive it with gratitude because it greatly strengthens them and kindles their love for God and neighbor, they should neither prolong their prayer beyond the time that has been set aside for it nor return to prayer only to enjoy this experience. For we must seek God, not our own delight. However, because of the good fruits it produces in them and the effective help it gives them for serving God, it is fully legitimate for them later on to return to prayer for a while, so long as their duties do not prevent them from doing so.

According to St. Teresa of Jesus, the attitude of persons who pray in this way should be one of simple attention to God's presence (along with one or another affection or petition) and of enjoying this rest in God, without tiring themselves with many words or concepts, or with attempts to summon back the memory or imagination when the latter have slipped away. It is enough for them to redirect their inner gaze on the one who is favoring them, for their memory and imagination to be drawn inward again. This they will soon learn by experience. And they will also observe that they can by no means produce this state themselves. Their prayer will sometimes return to a level of mere watching and they will have to be content with a simple gaze that is more or less accompanied by affections. The fact that they have experienced that other kind of happiness and quiet will make the experience of their own powerlessness even more painful, but their humility (knowledge of the truth) will be greatly strengthened by it.

Through these experiences, the disciples of Christ will be fortified to no small degree in fidelity to the gospel. Of course they continue manifesting their imperfections, but now they almost spontaneously perform difficult acts of generosity, forgiveness for offenses, love of neighbor and humility. The love they feel for God intensifies, their devotion to Christ grows and their devotion to the mother of Jesus and his friends may return with a greater tenderness than before. Remember that prayer and life necessarily go together.

I would like to go back to and expand on the comparison we drew between the various degrees of prayer and what happens in interpersonal relationships of human friendship or love. We remarked that we could better understand the infused prayer of recollection by comparing it with our instinctive tendency to sympathetically identify with some special person and to focus our attention on him or her. We may likewise gain a better understanding of the prayer of quiet by comparing it to the first shared joys of human friendship or love. In these instances, even before we have reached the level of intimacy, we already experience joy in our relationship, a quiet joy of delighting in the other's presence and an ease at spending time in his or her company. Of course, this comparison is just as weak as the previous one, because no human relationship can come anywhere near influencing our psyche as deeply and powerfully as the experience of God does.

The Prayer of Simple Union

If the period characterized by infused recollection is often brief, that of the prayer of quiet usually lasts longer and tends to be interspersed sometimes with spells of painful aridity.

The degree of prayer that follows is called the prayer of "simple" union, because, beginning with it, all further degrees of prayer are degrees of ever deepening and more total union. What this prayer consists in is revealed by its very name: it consists in God's uniting the soul to the divine, leaving it in passivity and communicating the divine life to it. It is called "simple" only in comparison with the degrees of union that follow it. Its fundamental characteristic is an awareness that all of the inner faculties, from the will and understanding to the imagination, are being taken over. Those who pray this prayer no longer perceive just the effects of the divine presence (quiet and joy), but rather experience an act of possession and submission of their psyche. They feel dominated and possessed by God.

It is, then, above all an experience of passivity and a total rendering of oneself to the action of God. The will is not only drawn and set to rest, but united to the divine good pleasure. In contradistinction to what had happened to it in the prayer of quiet, the human being is now highly alert and invigorated, aflame in the living flame of God's love. Here, in comparison with what it was in the prayer of quiet, the perception of the divine presence is strong and overpowering.

Those who experience it are left with a diffuse sense of the presence of God in the depth of their being. It sometimes seems to them that they are deeply united with God's will yet are at the same time capable of handling the affairs of everyday life or of the ministry. They also often feel God surrounding them. St. Teresa affirms something that other witnesses have experienced: God becomes their dwelling place, their only true homeland.[16] They only feel "at home" in God.

Although these experiences of union last but a short while in comparison with those of quietude, they leave those who receive them with a great sense of certitude. If they may have had some doubts about their previous experiences, no doubt is possible about these, at least while they are having them. But then, neither is the soul inclined to reflect much about what it has or ceases to have.

Nothing more than this can be said, because the deeper and more total the experience is, the less can its various aspects be distinguished. The principal effect of these graces is to greatly enamor the believer, intensifying his or her love for God and increasing his or her generosity toward the neighbor. Those who have this experience feel habitually and forcibly drawn by truth, sincerity, generosity and beauty. For them, the whole world begins to vibrate with love. And of course it is now easier for them to find God in creatures.

During these experiences, the bodily senses remain awake, although they are not consciously adverted to nor can access be had through them. "This experience comes about in such a way," writes Teresa of Jesus, "that one cannot even stir the hands without a lot of effort. The eyes close without one's wanting them to close; or if a person keeps them open, he or she sees hardly anything . . . hears but does not understand what she or he hears."[17] If we were to attempt to attract the attention of the person by calling or touching him or her during the brief period that this experience lasts, it would cost him or her a very great effort to emerge from his or her state and attend to anything that was said to him or her.

Ecstatic Union

Simple union is followed by a still more powerful and total experience of union, one so powerful that it produces a loss of the external senses. The person is so deeply in the God who acts within that communication with the outside world is cut off. While this experience lasts, the person finds it impossible, not just difficult, to regain ordinary consciousness.

What constitutes this degree is, then, a most powerful experience of being united to God by God's taking possession of the human spirit. The loss of the senses is only a consequence and exterior reflection of this union. For clearly, although the human spirit can be ever more closely united to God, the bodily senses, since they are material, are not the passive term of union, but simply bear the consequences of what is happening within.

The mind is flooded with light. It seems as if God had suddenly lifted it up before a window to show it a marvelous landscape. The landscape is God, although seen and savored as in a reflection. During the ecstasy, there can be imaginative visions or imageless visions of a purely intellectual type. The will feels totally inflamed with love and quite happy. There may be rapid movements of the heart, sudden and powerful surges, stabs and wounds of love. The soul feels the superhuman power of the experience of love and thus feels wounded, but this brings it immense happiness.

Ecstasy may come on gradually, so that all of the senses are not lost at once. An inability to speak comes over one, and little by little the other faculties are lost. At the peak of the experience the extremities may grow cold. At other times ecstasy is sudden. It comes at once and with great force.

The senses are suspended because of their weakness. Ecstasy is at once caused by the power of the interior experience and the weakness of that part of the psyche and body that remain without energy. It appears to be somewhat similar to what happens in a trance or semi-trance brought about by natural factors. There are weak psyches which lose communication with the outside world, under the influence of their imaginations and fantasies. Some persons who have suffered a grave trauma remain for several hours without knowing what is going on around them. They can travel to one or more places without realizing where they are or registering it in their memory.

The likeness is only relative, however, because ecstasy (it should really be called "enstasy," being within oneself) is produced by an experience of love and is therefore without trauma. The soul is inwardly burning in a flame of godly love. Images need not intervene in ecstasy (although ecstasy can accompany an imaginative vision). What is always intensified is the perception of the divine presence and the experience of being seized by the Spirit and united to God.

Some mystics have been characterized by the great number and length of their ecstasies. Ordinarily they have also been visionaries, that is, they have enjoyed numerous visions accompanied by images and have had conversations with supernatural beings. Contrariwise, there have been other mystics in whom ecstasy or the loss of their senses has been less visible, and has come to them in the midst of a long session of prayer, at its most intense moment. Just as in the prayer of simple union (characterized by a painful difficulty to return to the outer world) a person engaged in it may simply appear to be quiet and absorbed in self, so an ecstasy may not be noted by the rest, and perhaps not even by the person in ecstasy, as long as he or she is in it. He or she will indeed note the greater intensity of union with God and a greater passivity in the experience. This explains why there are mystics who do not seem to have passed through this experience, either because they themselves did not consider speaking of their inner experience or because others do not seem to have noticed it.

This period of the spiritual life is characterized by a variety of interior experiences that are at once cognitive and volitional, all of which have one overall meaning: God's self-gift to the human being, with a promise of a fuller giving at a later time. God appears once more as the God of the promise, that is to say, the God who announces the better future precisely in God. Teresa of Jesus with her nuptial imagery (the most adequate imagery to represent mystical experience) speaks of a marriage promise, which in her society was a very serious matter. God in some sense enters into a commitment with us. This is usually marked by a vision in which women have a ring placed on their finger, or in which both men and women feel as if Christ placed his heart in place of their own.

The Christian man or woman comes forth from the ecstatic union immensely strengthened in spirit. Their whole heart is set on God and nothing else matters to them.[18] They would like to spend all their energies serving God.[19]

9

Prayer in the Dark

People who skim through the records left us by the mystics, without really reflecting on them, often come away with a false idea of the development of religious experience at this deeper level. The ordinary Christian generally believes that the mystic moves in a light-filled world. Yet the itinerary of the mystic seems to be marked much more by darkness than by light. Or, to put it more exactly, Christian mystics are much more frequently left blinded by the force of the powerful light that is communicated to them in their experience.

There are two main reasons for this widespread misunderstanding. First and foremost, it happens that a large part of the commonly held image of mystical experience is derived from the experience of that considerable group of men and women who have been at once mystics and visionaries or seers: people who have seen many imaged appearances, and have heard words or whole discourses from the heavenly personages who have appeared to them in prayer. Mystics (in this case mystic-visionaries), like their non-mystical visionary cousins, seem to live more among angels and saints than among the rest of us poor sinners who make up the community of Jesus' disciples. But as we have already remarked, being a mystic and being a visionary are two diverse things, although the two rather frequently occur in the same person.

The second cause for this confusion comes from the fact that mystics (even those who are not seers) ordinarily narrate and describe only the peak moments of their experiences in prayer when the presence of God seems to overwhelm them. More often than not, the things we refer to as the "diaries" of the mystics are simply scattered notes on these often light-filled and joyful moments, and not really diaries, in the sense of a book in which a Christian daily or almost daily describes the course of his or her prayer life throughout a certain period. If in fact we had a real *diary* to look at, we would soon discover that by and large the prayer of the Christian mystic, at least before he or she has reached the final stages of prayer, consists of simply "being there" silently in God's presence, dimly perceived, receiving no further response than that of the mysterious presence of God before the believer. We would discover that often this presence is not even felt. Teresa of Jesus states: "There are some souls . . . who, brought by our Lord to perfect contemplation, would like to be in that prayer always; but that is impossible. Yet this favor of the Lord remains with them in such a way that afterward they cannot engage as before in discursive thought about the mysteries of the Passion and life of Christ."[1] In her *Way of Perfection* she suggests that by the time she was writing it, in 1556, the Lord was sometimes absent.[2] Only in the Seventh Mansion the "person walks continually in an admirable way with Christ,"[3] without interior trials or feelings of dryness.[4] But even in this last mansion, there were stronger and weaker moments.

This darkness or silence of God forms a much greater part of the prayer life of Christian mystics than peak moments of perception do. Moreover, this darkness or silence only thickens in the measure that they advance along the way of experience and become increasingly aware of facing the divine mystery more directly at each new step. For the fact is that every mystical experience they have, despite all the light and joy it may bring, only serves to show them the incompleteness of all their experiences. God always eludes us; God remains inevitably beyond us. The light that reaches us is only a ray that emanates from a most luminous reality that we cannot perceive, the distant splendor of a city hidden beyond the horizon.

The Night of the Spirit

But there comes a moment when the mystic finds himself or herself walking along in darkness "like a blind man groping his way with hands, not eyes." It is a period of deepest suffering. All the well-known symbols of God seem to have dried up and been scattered by the wind. All the masks we had made to hang on the facelessness of God, so that we might perceive God in our fashion and likeness, now lie broken on the ground. Now all our concepts of God strike us as empty and void of meaning. The contemplative feels an immense love for God which takes the form of the keenest pangs of nostalgia and suffering. The reason is, that the mystic feels abandoned by "his" or "her" God. He or she undergoes strong temptations against faith and hope, and sometimes even urgings to hate and blaspheme God; and all of this is felt excruciatingly. Where are the lights and joys of yesteryear, the former awareness of being loved? It all seems to have been an illusion. Or at least there is the fear of having lost it all through sin. Their prayer—endless dryness and total emptiness—becomes a fearful thing to them.

John of the Cross has described this period as "the night of the spirit."[5] The darkness and absence penetrate to the very root of the mystic's being, his or her "spirit." The theologians of spirituality agree with John in insisting that the fact that this "night" is not simply a purification of the faculties of the soul (understanding, will and imagination), but a much more radical purification of one's very being (the self). The created subject is being prepared by the Spirit to be united to the infinite being we call God.

This experience of darkness occurs before the final degree of union: the transforming union.[6] Teresa of Jesus, who does not use the expression "night" and does not assign it a special "dwelling place" in the Interior Castle, nevertheless refers to the keen sufferings of the contemplative in her "sixth dwelling-place," where she treats of the ecstatic union, expressly singling out her longing for God, persecutions, sicknesses, being misunderstood by her confessor, mental darkness, fear that it had all been illusion, and feelings of her own ingratitude and misery.[7] Note that Teresa talks of these aspects of the "night" both before and after she deals with the most visible phenomenon of the ecstatic union, namely, ecstasy.

Two Interpretations or Two Modes

We have been talking of the "night of the spirit" as if it were a neatly distinct period of development in union with God. In so doing, we have followed the commonly held opinion. We say "commonly" because around the beginning of this century one theologian, the French Jesuit, Auguste Poulain, in his celebrated book *The Graces of Interior Prayer*, defended the position that the night of the spirit is nothing more than the negative or dark side of the prayers of quiet, simple union and ecstatic union, to the extent that these states contain elements of darkness and are the cause of sufferings or are interspersed with sufferings.[8] Poulain has had no followers with respect to this interpretation. The reason is that John of the Cross describes the sufferings of this night in such fearful images, comparing them to the pains of purgatory and even hell, that it is impossible to identify them with the darkness and associated sufferings of the simple or ecstatic union. The distinct experiences of the simple or ecstatic union are in themselves luminous and ordinarily cause much more joy than sorrow, although between the one and the other the soul may remain in darkness. Witnesses who have passed through this night (Angela of Foligno, Catherine of Genoa, Marie of the Incarnation) describe at least one distinct phase toward the end of their itinerary which has all the characteristics attributed to the dark night of the spirit. Nevertheless, we should listen to what Fr. Poulain had to say, because while it is certain that this night is caused by a person's being flooded by a light so intense as to leave him or her blind, it is also clear that every contemplative experience has an aspect of incompleteness and obscurity which thrusts the believer before the divine transcendence, which in turn brings both a feeling of personal powerlessness and an intense longing to draw closer to God. All mystical contemplation is thus in some sense a night, although in the distinct experiences of simple and ecstatic union the joyful and luminous side usually predominates. Every contemplative experience purifies the soul and prepares it for the next degree of union.

Thus it is not surprising that in a number of Christians this passive purification is brought about through these contemplative experiences, interspersed with briefer periods of suffering, although it is hard to detect in them a distinct, clear-cut period of "night of the spirit," with the very keen sufferings that ordinarily characterize it. But it is also certain that the great witnesses of the spirit pass through a period of dense night. The theologians of Christian spirituality commonly hold that this period of intense trial is necessary in order to arrive at the transforming union, with the implication that those who do not pass through this particularly painful phase do not reach the transforming union. This seems to clash with the fact that in many canonized saints, although some obvious mystical graces have been discovered in them, it is not possible to perceive any distinct period of passive purification such as described by St. John of the Cross. Those who are convinced that the full development of the Christian life necessarily issues in mystical experience have to ask themselves whether the passive purification of the spirit must perforce take on those forms described by the Spanish mystic. One can certainly raise the question of whether all canonized saints must have arrived at the transforming union. Theoretically it is not necessary, because what the church discusses and judges when it is preparing to beatify a Christian is whether that person has lived the gospel with a degree of intensity "above the ordinary, even among fervent Christians." This is the traditional definition of what until a short time ago used to be called "heroic virtue." But this does not require that the person in question should have reached the ultimate degree of Christian maturity, that is, the transforming union. It has always been held that there are degrees among the saints, "as star differs from star in brightness."

Yet this theoretical possibility cannot be invoked in order to explain the absence of a distinct period of profound passive purification in the life of not a few saints. This is so, not only because we cannot set ourselves to comparing the various degrees of faith, hope and love which the different men and women servants of God have reached, since the church itself has always refused to do this, leaving it to "the one who searches hearts," but also because there are men and women saints who toward the end of their life seem to be totally immersed in the grace of God with the characteristics attributed to the transforming union, despite the fact that we cannot identify in their lives that distinct period of profound and prolonged purification that John of the Cross describes. There are certainly several servants of God whose interior experiences have remained forever hidden, observed only in their outward reflection. But others have left us some record of their intimate experiences, yet we cannot find anything of their passing through the night of the spirit in the sense described above. Perhaps we may have to confess that the divine Spirit does not allow herself to be caught so readily in our tidy schemes.

We find some confirmation of this simply by glancing at the lives of those mystics who went through a night similar to the ones described by St. John of the Cross. Jeanne Françoise Frémyot de Chantal suffered greatly during the last seven or eight years of her life, and these sufferings did not cease until a month before her death. Marie of the Incarnation went through three phases of the night, one when she was twenty-five, another when she was thirty-one shortly after entering the convent, and a third which lasted for eight years, when she was already in her forties. John of the Cross himself ended his life persecuted and ostracized by the superiors of his order. It is hard not to see in this the exterior aspect of one phase of his night. Paul of the Cross, a unique case, lived in the densest darkness of faith for forty-five years. Later, we will have to come back to these last two cases.

Nature and Cause

It would not be amiss for us to reflect again on the nature of this radical purification of the human being.

John of the Cross has explained the cause of this painful experience. It is none other than an intensifying and radicalizing of the divine Spirit's action in the believer. Darkness of the understanding is caused by the faith and gifts of wisdom and understanding that take radical possession of the contemplative: God then appears in transcendence and the believer is invited to submit himself or herself totally to the mystery of God in the darkness of faith. But this darkness is caused precisely by the excess of light that floods the person. Precisely because the mystic is nearer to God than ever before and more immersed in the divinity, he or she senses the inadequacy of all representations of God and the infinite distance that separates Creator from creatures. One can approach God only in the purity of faith. The feeling of abandonment and the experience of one's own frailty are caused by hope, which is now truly revealed as hope in God's mercy, with no support in our merits. The sense of sorrow at one's distance is the result of the burning charity that leads the Christian to seek God alone, beyond oneself. This night is thus a positive experience, although the believer perceives it as negative; but it is an experience of God in divine transcendence and sovereignty.

The god we have fabricated dies, while the living and true God looks down on us with infinite condescension. The human being suffers, because this drying up and falling away of these images of God and this realization of the limitedness of every concept about the divinity go against the deepest tendencies of our psyche, which operates with images and concepts and finds security in them. What is in fact nearness and immersion is perceived as absence and emptiness. And all previous experiences are beset with doubts. Now, when we are truly beginning to be theologians ("God-knowers"), we are left without a theology. Moreover, this contact with the transcendent mystery of God gives us a terribly clear awareness of our creatureliness and of our own moral frailty. These are the times when the mystic feels most keenly his or her own sinfulness.[9]

These two elements, darkness of mind and a sense of God's absence, on the one hand, and a keen awareness of one's own frailty, on the other, seem to be the two most fundamental traits of the night of the spirit. In many cases, other painful phenomena have been noted, such as the ones we referred to above: urges to rebel against God, temptations against faith or to blasphemy, etc.

This is not a matter of God's withdrawing rather capriciously in order to put the fidelity of those who seek the face of God to the test. Rather, the "night" comes from the normal development of religious experience. It is a consequence of growing in faith. Through it the mystic is left greatly enriched and enlightened. The night is his or her profound and definitive purification.[10] It is this purgative aspect that most frequently comes to the fore. As we shall presently see, the "night" has a still broader meaning; but even this purification or purgation must itself be understood in its overall purpose and scope. Not only is it a purging of the mystic's defects, but also of his or her very being with its deepest tendencies, in order to leave room for God.

In this transcending of everything, and in the first place of their very selves so that they may be immersed in the divine mystery, both Christian and Muslim mystics seem, although with essential differences, to agree with the masters of Buddhism. A Renaissance Christian master little-cited today, the Benedictine abbott of Liesse, Louis de Blois (Blosius), described the situation of all mystics quite well (although he was speaking only about Christians) when he wrote: "Upon entering the desert of divinity, the soul finds itself happily lost."[11]

The Night and the Cross

Speaking of the labors that fall upon contemplatives, Teresa of Jesus expounds them expressly in relation to the passion of Christ. According to Teresa, the end and aim of the great favors bestowed on the mystics is to strengthen them in order to be able to imitate Christ in his sufferings.[12] The Poor Clare, Angela of Foligno, wrote: "The friends of the Father follow His Son. Their eyes are always fixed on the Beloved. The love of God impels them to retrace the way of the Cross."[13] Applying this to the sufferings of the night of the spirit, it is clear that this night fundamentally entails a sense of communion with the Redeemer and of intercession on behalf of the Church and humankind. The cross of Christ pervades and presides over the whole way of spirituality.

In some exemplary Christians, the night of the spirit is marked particularly by this sense of sharing in the sufferings of the Redeemer for the good of his church. We might mention three groups of men and women servants of God in whom this sense of being burdened with trials appears in high relief. In the first place there are those who have felt called by God in a special way to a life of reparation for the sins of the world. The author of this book has personally studied the case of Esperanza González, a Spanish mystic of the nineteenth century who founded the Congregation of the Handmaidens of the Heart of Mary. She felt called to spend her life in reparation and in intercession for the church. Her "night" lasted for twenty-five years and was marked by the most acute sufferings. In the few years that passed between her entry into the transforming union and her death, she continued to suffer a number of trials. In the second place there are those who, by the grace of God, have made the Lord's passion and death the explicit center of their spirituality. A clear example of this is Paul of the Cross who, after entering the transforming union, lived for forty-five years in great desolation and with a sense of being abandoned. In the third place there are those Christians who have been called to work intensely for the church and the human race. In this group we have Anthony Claret, who dedicated his life intensely to evangelization. After spending his life between the pendulum-swing of prayer and ministry, he discovered the way to overcome the antinomy between action and contemplation in the passion of Christ. Com-passion ("co-suffering") with the Redeemer is the supreme form of contributing to the good of the Church. It is significant that Vincent de Paul entered the night of the spirit after offering himself to God on behalf of a doctor of the Sorbonne who could not cope with doubts concerning faith.

The fact that some saints have gone back to traverse sufferings that are typical of the night of the spirit even after they have reached the transforming union (Marie of the Incarnation, among others) shows us that in its most fundamental, deepest sense, the night implies a communion with Christ crucified.

Prayer in a Limit-Situation

What is the contemplative's prayer like in the night of the spirit? Ordinarily, except in those isolated cases when the sun flashes for a moment through the storm-clouds, the prayer of the mystic in this state consists of acts of total faith in the incomprehensible God, of hope despite everything, of love that trembles between desires for God and laments over God's absence. Remember that during this time the believer is often beset by temptations against faith and hope, and occasionally by impulses toward hatred and blasphemy.

Catherine of Genoa has written that what makes this trial the hardest is the fact that mystics do not feel as if it is coming from God, for this would suffice to assure them of acting in conformity with God's saving will.[14] However, they believe, on the contrary, that it is all due to their own sins. Recall, too, that at this time the sense of one's own impurity is at its keenest. In fact God is so hidden—as Catherine herself comments—as not even to be perceived as the cause of this trial. Teresa adds that the Christian finds himself or herself as if in a desert, and applies the words of Psalm 102:8 to this situation: "I watch, and am as a sparrow alone upon the housetop"—alone above everything created, yet without the companionship of God. This, she adds, is "an extreme solitude." The soul asks itself, "Where is your God?" (Ps 42:4). What we have here is (to use Karl Jaspers' phrase) a limit-situation in which the believer can no longer find support in creatures, yet is left, apparently, without God.

In this situation, not a few of Christ's disciples turn their eyes to the Crucified, in order to find an explanation for their own state. The gospels themselves do something akin to this. In the fourth gospel's account of the last supper, the evangelist puts a long prayer on the lips of Jesus as a kind of conclusion to his life and ministry. Luke presents Jesus on the cross as the Son who commits his spirit to the Father in an act of filial love. Mark, in his terribly stark way, followed here by Matthew, presents Jesus crucified and praying in a limit-situation which he can only hope to overcome through recourse to prayer. However, his prayer seems to have lost all meaning. This is underscored by the other actors in the drama who, like the chorus in a Greek tragedy, comment on the meaning of the central action, sometimes quite wrongly. When Jesus cries out his great "Eli, Eli," they comment: "Leave him alone. Let's see whether Elijah comes to his rescue." Since Jesus is nailed to the cross, incapable of moving and guarded by soldiers, only God or someone sent by God can free him.

In this limit-situation, Jesus has in fact turned to prayer, crying out, according to Mark and Matthew:

My God, my God, why have you forsaken me?

The citing of the first verse of a psalm was sometimes used to insinuate that the person pronouncing it was reciting that psalm. This particular psalm continues:

far from my prayer, from the words of my cry?
O my God, I cry out by day, and you answer not;
by night, and there is no relief for me (Ps 22:2–3).

In order to understand these sentiments which Mark and Matthew attribute to Jesus, we must remember that the handing over of Jesus to the Romans ("dogs and swine") by the authorities of the people of God was equivalent to excommunicating him, to uprooting him and casting him out of the religious community of his people. He was now neither a Jew nor a Gentile. The cross itself seemed to stand between him and God, according to the customary interpretation of Deuteronomy 21:23: "God's curse rests on him who hangs on a tree." Everything seemed to have failed. The message had been rejected, the messenger had been executed, the disciples had been scattered and Jesus now found himself on the threshold of the land of the dead, "where no one praises God." In the Hebrew scriptures, death was tantamount to the absence of God.

In this limit-situation, Jesus addresses himself to "his

God." It was not a matter of his asking God to take him down from the cross, as the bystanders thought. For although the first half of Psalm 22 is a petition for help, it changes into an act of thanksgiving in the second half. But it seems that Mark, at least, does not mean to attribute this intention to Jesus. For Mark, Jesus on the cross is the powerless and abandoned Christ. His prayer remains a pure lament, consisting of a holding up of his sorrowful situation to compare it to the will of God.

This is exactly the prayer of the Christian mystic in the no-exit situation of the night of the spirit. The mystic does not ask to be freed from it, but simply wishes to hold up his or her situation to compare it to the loving will of God, to discover where God is in all of this. It is a prayer—that of Jesus and that of the mystic—which consists of trying to discover the Presence in the absence—an act of pure faith.

The Night of Jesus

The prayer of Jesus on the cross suggests to us that we should probe more deeply into his state as described in this first interpretation of the passion—the one that Mark (followed by Matthew) gives us.

If Isaiah had called God "a God who concealed himself" (Is 45:15), the gospel of Mark presents Jesus as the just man who feels abandoned by God. Jesus adopts as his own the sentiments of the "poor" ('ânî) of Psalm 22:25, of the just man who complains to God because he feels that God is far away from him in his moment of greatest need. This is what we had in mind in the heading of the preceding section of this chapter, "Prayer in a Limit-Situation." That the apostolic church saw the sorrowful image of the Crucified shining through Psalm 22 is confirmed by the obvious parallels it drew between other verses of the psalm and the account of the crucifixion of Jesus.

This powerfully moving image of the God-forsaken

Messiah seems to have been fraught with serious difficulties for Luke. Therefore, whereas Matthew repeats the Markan lament (Mt 27:46), Luke suppresses it and instead cites another psalm as the last prayer of Jesus: "Into your hands I commend my spirit" (Lk 23:46; Ps 31:6), prefacing it with the invocation "Father!" which is not found in the 31st Psalm. Thus, according to Luke, the cross does not seem to pose any obstacle between the humanity of Jesus and the divine mystery. In Mark, however, it surely does so. In Gethsemani, Jesus had called on God as his *Abba,* asking him to free him from the impending crisis (Mk 14:36). The invocation of God as *Abba* certainly reflected the intimate awareness Jesus had of his coming forth from God. But at the same time it was a transposition of a quite human experience that Jesus had had during his infancy and adolescence. For the humanity of Jesus was used to invoking God the same way he had once addressed Joseph. He was, then, projecting on the faceless mystery of the divinity the loving face with which Joseph had looked out for him and the firm hand with which Joseph had supported and fed him. Now, on the cross, the face of Joseph disappears, and Jesus calls upon the divine mystery with the name of "God." "God" refers to the divine reality as transcendent and mysterious. It is by that very fact a vague name without any familiar contours. It does not designate the divinity by one of God's intelligible (?) attributes, such as "merciful," "all-knowing" or "almighty," nor does it even explicitly express a personal relationship, as the terms "Lord," "Creator" and "Father" do. God is simply God. Now although we are not trying to attribute an explicit intention to Mark, it is clear that he who transmits the prayer of Jesus in the garden using Jesus' invocation of his *Abba,* prefers, when presenting Jesus on the cross, to attribute to him the prayer of the just man to the "God" who has abandoned him.

We cannot understand this situation of Jesus adequately unless we take our starting point from a fully orthodox christology. If Jesus is radically "of God" and "in

God's presence," if his being is defined in its depth by his unique relationship with God, and if it is certain that because of this God is revealed definitively in Jesus, it is likewise certain that, since Jesus is truly and fully man, the divinity infinitely surpasses his humanity and therefore that the humanity of Jesus not only reveals but also conceals the divine mystery.

While Jesus manifested a profound respect for the mysterious sovereignty of God throughout his life, giving thanks for God's decisions (Mt 11:25–26) and submitting his most intimate desires to the will of his *Abba* (Mk 14:36), it was above all on the cross that he stood naked and powerless before the mystery. All of the symbols he had used to refer to God now lay broken at the foot of the cross. All that remained was the neutral name of God and a lament, "why have you abandoned me?" At this moment, more than ever before, Jesus livingly experienced the divine transcendence, the absolute incapacity of all humanity to embrace God and hold God captive in our concepts and representations. God's ways are not our ways. The messenger of God's definitive grace now finds himself repudiated by the authorities of his people (his religion) and feels abandoned by God. Jesus feels near to death, which in his Jewish culture and for himself meant the void of God, the absence of that God who is the God of the living and not of the dead, as he himself had remarked to the Sadducees (Mt 22:32). Jesus, whose ministry had consisted of putting God on the side of those who apparently had no God (publicans and other public sinners), is now dying as the publican par excellence, outcast and excommunicated. The passion was Jesus' night of the spirit.

And yet, although he did not feel it, God was sustaining him in faith. In a crucial and possibly apocalyptic aside, Mark tells us that when Jesus died, the veil of the temple was torn in two from top to bottom. We now know what was in the sanctuary. Flavius Josephus describes for us the surprise of the Romans when they entered it in the year 70: it was an empty room. God, we would add, was with Jesus, suffering with him. His glorified humanity would henceforth be the new temple.

When Angela of Foligno and Teresa of Jesus (among others) spoke of the sufferings of contemplatives as a sharing in the sufferings of the crucified Son of God, they were talking above all of the desire of mystics to be assimilated to Christ. In reality, independently of any subjective attitude on the part of the disciple, it is clear that he or she is in some way reliving the trial to which the Master was submitted. Catherine Emmerich, who was famed not only for her visions of the passion but also for having drawn attention to the supernatural in the heyday of German romanticism, dramatically expressed the situation of complete abandonment in which the Redeemer found himself by her statement that in this way Christ obtained for us the strength to overcome the sufferings that arise from feeling totally abandoned.[15] There can be no doubt that Christ obtained strength for us. But his going through seems, moreover, in keeping with what we have said, to have been an exemplar and prototype. Jesus himself went through the night of the spirit that so many men and women mystics would later have to go through.

10

You Shall Love the Lord Your God with All Your Heart

The fullness of love is the goal of the entire development of Christian life. The commandment to love God with all our heart and our neighbor as ourselves is in fact more than just another goal set before us: it is our vocation. Yet spiritual theology has traditionally and repeatedly told us that in our earthly journeying toward this vocation, few, indeed very few, even among the most chosen, reach the perfection of love to which we are called. The reason is that what we can do ourselves, with God's grace, is not enough to carry us to this point. Besides this, it is necessary that grace itself purify and broaden our heart. And this is the work assigned to the purification that we call "the night of the spirit."

Once this trial has been accomplished, the believer goes forth from God's hands to this final stage of perfect love. Angela of Foligno calls it the third and final degree of union in which the soul is united to God and God is united to the soul.[1] John of the Cross, following this tradition, calls it the "'transforming union." Teresa of Jesus tells us that these are the innermost mansions of the Interior Castle, where God dwells, creating us and lifting us up to the divine Being itself: the believer at last enters so deeply into the self as to encounter the very source of his or her being. It is a matter of going as far as possible in a wayfarer's anticipation (for they have still not entered into the vision of glory) of communion with God in eternity.

It is indeed a "union" with God, but in order to distinguish it from the two lower degrees of contemplative union (simple and ecstatic), it is called "transforming union." Three fundamental characteristics mark this union. Above all, it is no longer just a matter of the union of the faculties, as when God took hold of the understanding and the will, making them taste in a transitory way the presence and action (simple union), with such force that even the senses were lost in the experience (ecstatic union). In this final stage, the very created *self* is united to the divinity in a radical way. God, as Marie of the Incarnation testifies, "takes possession of the soul to the extent of converting it in the very ground of its substance."[2] Christian tradition, both in the east and west, has frequently cited a text from St. Paul in order to explain this state: "The life I live now is not my own; Christ is living in me" (Gal 2:20). God, in the crucified and risen Christ, becomes the life of the believer.

In the second place, at this stage there is a mutual self-giving between God and the believer. Christian tradition, inspired by the Song of Songs, has called this union a "marriage," an image which the Spirit herself uses to describe God's covenant with Israel. It should be noted that the Muslim mystics also speak of the union between lover and beloved. This is because, in the view born of biblical and Islamic traditions (as opposed to the self-annulling ideal of Buddhism), the created being does not disappear even in this last degree of union.

Finally, in this transforming union God becomes the very life of the human being to such a degree as to become a constant object of experience. The communication of grace, the "sharing in the divine nature" (2 Pet 1:4), which has been infused in baptism by means of faith and the sacrament, now reaches such a degree that it becomes an experience of communion. It is significant that this is the time when mystical experiences focus especially on the mystery of the Trinity and are filled with the highest enlightenments on the incarnation. Evagrius talks of the "knowledge of the Holy Trinity" as the peak of Christian life.[3] This knowledge happens in intellectual visions, or visions without images, in which the intellect "sees" and the whole spirit experiences the divine Presence.

Even here, as in a musical composition, there are variations of intensity: moments of *fortissimo* and *pianissimo*. The strong moments are these high experiences of illumination, while the weak moments are so to speak the rest of the mystic's life, where the divine Presence is felt as an atmosphere that envelops and supports him or her. Often— very often—the human spirit will be drawn toward this Presence and turn its attention to God: "the soul finds itself in this company every time it takes notice."[4]

By this time, too, there is an end of ecstasies (which were the result of human weakness meeting the imperious force of grace), because the soul has now been deeply strengthened. Whereas the former states had been characterized by isolated, repeated experiences, now there is an habitual perception of the presence of God, both in the contemplative and in the world of which he or she forms a part. The believer finds himself or herself "firmly established in the truth," that is, in God.

The Just Live by Faith

Now, more than ever before, those disciples of Christ who have reached this stage are aware not only of their dependence on God for everything but also of their own frailty. Yet now, too, more than ever before, they commit themselves totally to God, living by God's word and grace. Their faith is so intense that it becomes an habitual experience of the divine transcendence. Thanks to the divine action that has prepared them for it, these believers at last let God be God in everything.

One hopes, in these days of difficult and sometimes troubled ecumenism, that Catholic readers will not think it odd that I have chosen the words of a great spiritual writer of another Christian church, John Wesley, in order to describe the behavior of a mystic who has allowed God to lead him or her to the transforming union. The Spirit is at work in all those who seek God sincerely. Wesley, speaking of the perfect Methodist (and we would add, of any perfect Christian), says:

> A *Methodist* is one who loves the Lord his God with all his heart, with all his soul, with all his mind, and with all his strength. God is the joy of his heart and the desire of his soul. . . . From him, therefore, he cheerfully receives all . . . into whose hands he has wholly committed his body and soul. . . .
>
> For indeed he *prays without ceasing.* . . . His heart is lifted up to God at all times, and in all places. In this he is never hindered, much less interrupted, by any person or thing. In retirement or in company, in leisure, business or conversation, his heart is ever with the Lord. . . .
>
> And loving God, he *loves his neighbor as himself;* he loves every man as his own soul. He loves his enemies, yea, and the enemies of God. . . . He is *pure in heart.* . . . *Whatsoever he does, it is all to the glory of God.*[5]

Mysticism, Morals and Prophecy

Some have set up an exaggeratedly rigorous opposition between the ethical element (doing the will of God) and the mystical element (union of the created being with God) in Christian life. The whole of Christian tradition has indeed affirmed that it is essential to do the will of God. But God is not only the ruler of our will; God is the Creator who is present in the very depth of our being, and the Spirit who moves us, teaches us to pray, and prays in us. Grace, the pure grace of God, keeps penetrating us progressively, until it unites our being with the divine being. Moreover, the ethical union of our will with God's will is itself oriented toward the union of our being, and this is realized perfectly in this union which we call mystical.

The same may be said of the distinction that has sometimes been made between the prophetic element and the mystical element in the Christian vocation—the implication being that the prophetic element is "biblical," whereas the mystical element is of suspect origin. Now, while there is good enough basis for distinguishing the prophetic and the mystical, the distinction is not one of mutual opposition or exclusion. The great Christian mystics (Francis of Assisi, Catherine of Siena, Teresa of Jesus, Charles de Foucauld) have often been great prophets, pointing out to the Church the ways of God. The fact is that the mystic often doubles as a prophet.

Effects

Let us now enumerate some of the principal effects that the transforming union causes in these high mystics.

First and foremost, since God has become the very center of their life of faith and love, they forget themselves totally and are fully above everything created. They seek only God, and not their own consolation, their own virtue or their own honor. Although they are fully aware of their having been healed and enriched in God, they desire only to serve God and have others serve God. Once again, the just live by faith.

In order to serve God and make others serve God, these Christians now find themselves endowed with great power, and this is the time when mystics develop an intense activity. When they reached this stage, Francis of Assisi, Catherine of Siena, Ignatius Loyola, Teresa of Jesus and Anthony Claret were all intensely committed to the service of God. Teresa and Anthony Claret undertook numerous journeys in order to fulfill God's will for them to write and orally proclaim the grace of God, but they did so while maintaining themselves habitually in the presence of God, without losing that peace which is the fruit of the Spirit. Martha and Mary, St. Anthony Claret tells us, are fused into a single person. The fact is that at this stage God is experienced as the very source of ministerial action and as dwelling in the neighbor who is ministered to. The mystic is now, to use the expression of Vincent de Paul, "passive in action." The experience of God's active presence is so great that the mystic tends to radiate it outwardly. Numerous testimonies of people who have dealt with a man or woman servant of God in this state (Dominic de Guzmán, Catherine of Siena, Francis de Sales) mention this.

This unalterable peace continues in the midst of outward contradictions and persecutions, because even here the cross of the Lord does not disappear. John of the Cross personally experienced this: he was persecuted even after his death by his own religious brethren. Anthony Claret died in utter poverty in a foreign country, after a group of Cistercians had charitably taken him into their monastery while he was being hunted down by the police. And it was at that time he received some special illuminations on the passion of the Lord and on Christ's love for his enemies.

Finally, during this stage the mystic enjoys a great power of intercession with God. When the Holy Spirit gives herself to our spirit, she also communicates to us her great power, the power of making intercession. But the very communion of the believer with God becomes itself an intercession, whether or not he or she is explicitly asking for anything, because the grace whereby God enriches the mystic also definitively enriches the church. The more immersed one is in God, the more one is in communion with humanity and the church. The mystic encounters the world and the church in God. There is no need, then, for the mystic, like the Boddhisattva in Buddhist legend, to renounce nirvana in order to continue along the compassionate way of drawing others upward and interceding for them. It is in total communion that one has the greatest power to draw and intercede. The letter to the Hebrews describes the glory of Christ as a constant intercession. A weak reflection of this occurs at this stage.

Cross and Glory

The Stoics described the wise as those who have reached ataraxy, that is, a tranquilization of the passions and a perfect stability of mind. Now while it is true that their passions have subsided, it is nonetheless true that believers who have reached the transforming union are still capable of suffering. In one way or another, our sharing in the cross of Christ never ceases in this life.

This happens in two ways. There have been a few men and women servants of God who seem to have gone back into a reparatory or intercessory night of the spirit, even after they have been brought to the transforming union. This seems to have happened to Marie of the Incarnation (seventeenth century). We suspect that the essential character of the transforming union remains even in these cases: the presence of God is habitually perceived, although this presence is a source of sufferings, while the more luminous experiences either disappear or occur very rarely.

In other cases, the contemplative experiences continue, but in the outer world the believer is assailed by all sorts of contradictions and unpleasantness. Teresa of Jesus tells us that this is what happened to her: "in every thing she found herself improved, and it seemed to her, despite the trials she underwent and the business affairs she had to attend to, that the essential part of her soul never moved from that room (God's inmost mansion). As a result it seemed to her that there was, in a certain way, a division in her soul. And while suffering some great trials a little after

God granted her this favor, she complained of that part of the soul, as Martha complained of Mary, and sometimes pointed out that it was there always enjoying that quietude at its own pleasure while leaving her in the midst of so many trials and occupations that she could not keep it company."[6]

Constant Amazement

But for all these sufferings, there is a deeper reason that prevents us from seeing in the transforming union something of the boring life of the romantic aristocrat enclosed in an ivory tower. And this reason is the constant admiration of the divine grandeur which the mystic experiences. St. Teresa has said as much: "Each day this soul becomes more amazed!"[7] And, we would add, not only because it seems that the divine presence never leaves it, but also because the contemplation, and above all the intense experiences it has, disclose to the soul the most unsuspected and fresh insights into the grandeur and beauty of God.

God is always infinite Being, and even after bringing a soul to this state of union, God always remains beyond its lights and concepts. Therefore the mystic is always overawed in the presence of the God who is revealed to him or her as the Ever Greater.

Gregory of Nyssa, one of the greatest masters of Christian mysticism, spoke of this constant discovery (epectasis) which according to him, not only mystics on earth experience, but also the blessed in heaven.[8] We go from light to light, and from amazement to amazement.[9] Gregory was inspired by Origen.[10] God, for the mystic, is always new and always surprising.

Notes

1: Approaching the Theme

[1]Philo of Alexandria, *The Life of Moses*, in *Works*, Loeb Classical Library (Cambridge: Harvard, 1966) VI, pp. 267–595. Gregory of Nyssa, *The Life of Moses*, trans. by A. J. Malherbe and E. Ferguson (New York: Paulist, 1978).

[2]Gregory of Nyssa, *De Orat Dominc.* I: PG 44, 1124, B–C. He seems to have borrowed this expression from Clement of Alexandria (*Stromata* 7, c. 7: PG 9, 456).

[3]Evagrius of Pontus, *Chapters on Prayer*, ch. 3: PG 79, 1168. Eng. version by J. E. Bamberger: *The Praktikos, Chapters on Prayer* (Spencer: Cistercian, 1970) p. 56. Clement, Gregory and Evagrius use the term *homilia* (conversation). John Chrysostom, on the contrary, defines prayer as *dialexis*, dialogue (*In Genesim* 30, 5: PG 53, 280).

[4]Jerome, *Ep.* 22.25: PL 22, 411.

[5]Augustine, *Serm.* 230 *de temp.* PL 39, 1886.

[6]John Climacus, PG 88, 1129, in *The Ladder of Divine Ascent*, Step 28 (New York: Paulist, 1982) p. 274.

[7]K. Rahner, *Encounters with Silence* (Westminster: Newman, 1963) pp. 19–20.

[8]Cyprian, Ep. I, 15: PL 4, 226.

[9]Augustine, In Ps. 85, 7: PL 37, 1086.

[10]Augustine, *Confessions*, V, 9, 17; trans. by V. J. Bourke (New York: The Fathers of the Church, 1953) p. 118.

[11]K. Rahner, *Encounters with Silence*, pp. 19–20. Cf.

also K. Rahner, "Prayer as Dialogue," in *The Practice of Faith*, 18 (New York: Crossroad, 1983) p. 94.

[12]Evagrius of Pontus, Chapters on Prayer, n. 3, in *The Praktikos and Chapters on Prayer* (Kalamazoo: Cistercian Pub., 1981) p. 56.

[13]*The Syrian Fathers on Prayer and the Spiritual Life* (Kalamazoo: Cistercian Pub., 1987) pp. 194–195.

[14]Origen, *De Orat.* 9, 2. In *An Exhortation to Martyrdom, Prayer and Selected Works* (New York: Paulist, 1979) p. 99.

[15]Augustine, Serm. 73: PL 39, 1187.

[16]Evagrius of Pontus, *Chapters on Prayer*, 35: PG 79, 1173. Eng. trans. *The Praktikos, Chapters on Prayer* p. 60.

[17]John Damascene, *De Fide Orthodoxa*, 3, 24: PG 94, 1089–1091. English trans. by F. H. Chase (New York: Fathers of the Church, 1958) p. 328.

[18]Augustine, *Confessions*, X, 27, n. 38; III, 6, n. 11: PL 32, 795, and 888. English trans. by V. J. Bourke (New York: The Fathers of the Church, 1953) pp. 297 and 60.

[19]William of Saint Thierry, *The Golden Epistle* (Kalamazoo: Cistercian, 1980) p. 67.

[20]Teresa of Jesus, *Life* 8, 5 in *Collected Works*, trans. by O. Rodriguez and K. Kavanaugh (Washington: ICS, 1980) I.

[21]Evagrius of Pontus, *Chapters on Prayer:* PG 79, 1168. Eng. trans. p. 56.

[22]John Cassian, *Coll.* 10, 71: PL 49, 828; Eng. trans. by O. Luibheid (New York: Paulist, 1985) pp. 129–130.

[23]Evagrius of Pontus, *Sententiae ad Virgines, 5:* PG 40, 1283. Cf. *The Sayings of the Desert Fathers*, trans. by B. Ward, Benjamin, 4 (Kalamazoo: Cistercian: 1975) p. 37.

[24]Bernard, *De modo vivendi*, Serm. 49: PL 184, 1271.

[25]Thomas de Celano, Leg. II, c. 61 in Saint Francis of Assisi, *Writings and Early Biographies* (Chicago: Franciscan Herald Press, 1972) p. 441.

[26]Augustine, Letter 130 to Proba, in *Letters*, The Fa-

thers of the Church, 18 (New York: The Fathers of the Church, 1953) pp. 387–388.

[27]Augustine, *Epist.* 194, 7: PL 33, 878.

[28]Evagrius of Pontus, *Chapters on Prayer*, 58: PL 79, 1180. Eng. trans. p. 64.

[29]Origen, *De Orat.* 2, 3: PG 11, 417–421. In *An Exhortation to Martyrdom . . .* p. 84.

[30]Augustine, *Epist.* 194, 16–18: PL 33, 880.

[31]Luther, Erl. 12, 160 on John 16, 23.

[32]Luther insists strongly on the need for constant prayer. Cf. *Treatise on Good Works*, "On the Third Commandment" nn. 7–8, trans. by W. A. Lambert, in *Works*, vol. 44 (Philadelphia: Fortress Press, 1973) pp. 61–62. He has some beautiful statements on how natural is prayer for Christians: "you cannot find a Christian without prayer, just as you cannot find a living person without a pulse. The pulse never stands still; it is always throbbing through and beating by itself. Even though a person is sleeping or doing something else and therefore he or she is not aware of it" (W 45, 541; Er 49, 114; SL 8, 363).

[33]Augustine, Epist. 130 to Proba, 8, 17: PL 33, 500–501; Eng. trans. *Letters* (New York: The Fathers of the Church, 1953) pp. 389–390.

[34]R. Llewelyn, *All Shall be Well. The Spirituality of Julian of Norwich for Today* (New York: Paulist, 1984) pp. 51–59.

[35]John and Charles Wesley, *Selected Writings and Hymns* (New York: Paulist, 1981) pp. 304 and 306.

[36]Teresa of Jesus, *The Way of Perfection*, 22.1 (37.1) and 24.4 (40.3). *The Collected Works* (Washington: ICS, 1980) vol. II, pp. 121–122 and 129.

[37]*Life* 8.5, vol. I, p. 67.

[38]*Life* 37,4, pp. 252–253.

[39]*Way*, 16.6 (26.3), II, p. 95.

[40]*Way*, 26.9, II, p. 136.

[41]Thomas Aquinas, 2–2 q. 23, a. 1.

[42]*Life*, 7.21, I, p. 64.
[43]*Way*, 18.2 (28.3), II, p. 102.
[44]*Way*, 28.3 (46.3), II, p. 141.
[45]*Way*, 26.3 (42.3), II, pp. 133–134.
[46]*Way*, 16.6 (26.3). In the ICS edition: 16.10, II, p. 97.
[47]*Foundations*, 5.2, III, p. 116.
[48]*Int. Castle*, IV, 1.7, II, p. 319.
[49]*Ibid.*

2:   *Jesus and Prayer*

[1]The most extensive theological reflection on the prayer of Jesus has been made from the point of view of the theology of liberation: J. Sobrino, "The Prayer of Jesus and the God of Jesus in the Synoptic Gospels," *Listening*, Fall 1978, pp. 179–189.

[2]E. J. Fisher in *Spirituality and Prayer* (New York: Paulist, 1983) p. 140.

[3]J. Jeremias, *The Prayers of Jesus* (Philadelphia: Fortress, 1978).

[4]J. Jeremias, *Unknown Sayings of Jesus*, trans. by R. Fuller (London: SPCK, 1957), pp. 98–100.

3:   *Prayer and Life*

[1]D. Hassel, *Radical Prayer* (New York: Paulist, 1983) pp. 20–37.

[2]Evagrius of Pontus, *The Praktikos*, 2–3: PG 79, 1168. Eng. trans. pp. 15–16.

[3]Thomas Aquinas, 2–2, q. 188, a. 2.

[4]John of the Cross, *The Spiritual Canticle*, strophe 14.

[5]John of the Cross, *The Spiritual Canticle*, Commentary on Strophes 14–15, n. 8.

[6]P. Teilhard de Chardin, *La Messe sur le monde* (Paris: Seuil, 1965). On Teilhard cf. M. Kessler and B.

Brown, eds. *Dimensions of the Future: The Spirituality of Teilhard de Chardin* (Washington: Corpus Books, 1968).

[7]*De Orat.* 12: PG 11, 452. *Exhortation to Martyrdom*, pp. 104–105. *In Reg. Hom.* I. 9: PG 12, 1004–1005.

[8]*In Ps.* I.2: PG 12, 1088.

[9]*Constitutions S.J.*, III, 1.26.

[10]J. M. Lozano et al., *Ministerial Spirituality and Religious Life* (Chicago: Claretian, 1986). We would like to recommend in a particular way the chapters by Dianne Bergant "The Rebirth of an Apostolic Woman," pp. 73–99 and Mary Ellen Moore, "Psychoptherapy as Ministry," pp. 117–128. R. Haight has recently published an enlightening study on the Ignatian Spirituality in the light of action: *Foundational Issues in Jesuit Spirituality*, in *Studies in the Spirituality of Jesuits*, (Saint Louis) 19/4, September 1987.

[11]J. Nadal, in *Monumenta Nadal*, IV, pp. 651–652.

[12]Vincent de Paul, *Correspondence, Entretiens, Documents* (Paris, 1920–1925), VII, p. 38; I, p. 62; IV, p. 123.

4:   *The First Three Degrees of Prayer*

[1]J. W. Fowler, *Stages of Faith. The Psychology of Human Development and the Quest for Meaning* (San Francisco: Harper and Row, 1981).

[2]The contrary opinion seems to be suggested by J. Brewi and A. Brennan in their otherwise excellent book *Midlife: Psychological and Spiritual Perspectives* (New York: Crossroad, 1982) pp. 122–123.

[3]John of the Cross, *Ascent*, II, 22.3 in *Collected Works*, trans. by K. Kavanaugh O.C.D. and O. Rodriguez, O.C.D. (Washington: ICS, 1979) p. 179.

[4]*The Way*, 22.1 (37.1), II, pp. 121–122.

[5]*Meditationes Vitae Christi*, ch. 36.

[6]Teresa of Jesus, *Way*, 26.1, (42, 1), II, p. 133.

[7]*Way*, 24.3 (40.4), II, p. 129.

[8]*Life*, 22.3, I, p. 142.

[9]*Int. Castle*, VI, 7.5, II, p. 399.

[10]Gregory of Nyssa, *Life of Moses*, n. 248 (New York: Paulist, 1982).

[11]Bernard, *On the Song of Songs*, 61.7 (Kalamazoo: Cistercian, 1979) p. 146. Guerric of Igny, *Sermones in Dominica Palmis*, 4.5–6: PL 185.140–142.

[12]John of the Cross, *Canticle*, stanza 37.3 (Washington: ICS, 1979) pp. 550–551.

5: *Prayer and Crisis*

[1]J. Fowler, *Stages of Faith*, pp. 153–154.

[2]A. Brennan and J. Brewi, *Mid-Life Directions* (New York: Paulist, 1985).

[3]C. Fitzgerald, O.C.D., "Impasse and Dark Night," in T. H. Edwards, *Living with Apocalypse* (San Francisco: Harper and Row, 1983) pp. 93–116.

[4]B. Lane, "Spirituality and Political Commitment," *America*, March 14, 1981.

[5]John of the Cross, *Dark Night*, I, 8.1, p. 311.

[6]*Dark Night*, I, 8.1, p. 311.

[7]*Dark Night*, I, 8.4, p. 312.

[8]*Dark Night*, I, 10.2, p. 317.

[9]*Ascent*, II, 1.3, pp. 110–111.

[10]Baltasar Alvarez, *Escritos Espirituales* (Barcelona: J. Flors, 1961), p. 246.

[11]*Ibid.* p. 250, 1. 83, a. 1.

6: *Waiting for God*

[1]*Dark Night*, I, 10.2, p. 317.

[2]*Int. Castle*, IV, 3.5, II, p. 329.

[3]*Int. Castle*, II, 1.3, p. 329.

[4]*Ascent*, II, 22.3, p. 179.

[5]Baltasar Alvarez, *Escritos Espirituales* (Barcelona: J. Flors, 1961) pp. 207–208.

[6]*Ibid.* p. 244.

[7]John Damascene, *De Fide Orth.* III, 24: PG 94, 1098–1099; Eng. trans. by F. H. Chase (New York: The Fathers of the Church, 1958) p. 328. Thomas Aquinas, 2–2, q. 83, a. 1.

[8]Thomas Aquinas, 2–2, 1. 83.

[9]Bonaventure, *De Triplici Via.* Eng. trans. by W. J. Joffe, *The Inkindling of Love, also called The Triple Way* (Paterson: Saint Anthony Guild Press, 1956). Bonaventure, in our opinion, does not require that the three elements appear explicitly in every prayer. They may be implicitly present.

[10]*Ascent* II, 13.2–4, pp. 140–141.

[11]*Dark Night*, I, 8.4, p. 312.

[12]*The Cloud of Unknowing*, J. Walsh, ed. (New York: Paulist, 1981) p. 195.

[13]*Life*, 8.5, I. p. 67.

[14]*Way*, 16.6 (26.3). In ICS transl. 16.10, II, p. 97.

[15]*Way*, 26.3 (42.3), II, pp. 133–134.

[16]*Dark Night*, I, 10.4, p. 317.

[17]Baltasar Alvarez, *Escritos Espirituales*, p. 238.

[18]*Way*, 26.3 (42.3), II, pp. 133–134.

[19]Teresa of Jesus, *Life*, 24.3, I, pp. 159–150.

7: *Approaching Mystical Experience*

[1]The best known supporters of this opinions were A. Poulain, S.J. and the Carmelite theologians Crisogono de Jesus, Gabriele di Santa Maria Maddalena, and Silveria de Santa Teresa.

[2]Among the supporters of this opinion: M. Saudreau and the Dominicans A. Gardeil, Juan Gonzalez Arintero, R. Garrigou Lagrange, A. Royo Marin, and J. Aumann.

[3]*The Life of Anthony*, ch. 82: PG 26, 957. Eng. trans. by R. T. Meyer (Westminster: Newman, 1950) p. 87.

[4]Origen, *In Cant.*, prol.: PG 13, 76D.

[5]John Cassian, *Coll.* IX, 8 and 15: PL 49, 780, 786. Eng. trans. by O. Luibheid (New York: Paulist, 1985), pp. 107, 110.

[6]Gregory of Nyssa, *Hom.* 11 *In Cant.:* PG 44, 1000D.

[7]Pseudo Denis, *De Mystica Theologia*, PG 3, 1000D–1001A.

[8]John Cassian, *Coll.* IX, 18 and 26: PL 49, 788, 802. Eng. trans. pp. 111, 117.

[9]John Cassian, *Coll.* IX, 31: PL 49, 807. Eng. trans. p. 119.

[10]Bernard, *In Cant.* III, 5: PL 183, 985–986; Eng. trans. by K. Walsh, *On the Song of Songs* (Kalamazoo: Cistercian, 1976) I, pp. 19–20.

[11]Bernard, *In Cant.* XLI.3: PL 183, 985–986; Eng. trans. II, pp. 206–207.

[12]If we were asked to go further than this (although we would often be lacking documentation for our statements), we would have to classify Bernard of Clairvaux and probably Augustine among the great non-visionary mystics.

[13]Teresa of Jesus, *Int. Castle*, 3, 1.5, II, p. 306.

8: *The Higher Degrees of Prayer*

[1]Augustine, *Confessions*, X, 40, n. 65: PL 32, 806–807. Eng. trans. by V. J. Bourke (New York: The Fathers of the Church, 1953) pp. 320–321. *Enarr. in Ps.* 42.7: PL 36, 480–481.

[2]*The Syriac Fathers on Prayer and the Spiritual Life* (Kalamazoo: Cistercian, 1987) pp. 253–254. The idea of a state of non-prayer, or spiritual prayer, above the stage of pure prayer, was suggested to Isaac by John of Apamea and by a mistaken translation of Evagrius, *Capita cognoscitiva*, 30.

[3]C. Morris, *The Discovery of the Individual* (Toronto: University of Toronto Press, 1972).

[4]Bernard, *In Cant.* 3.1: PL 183, 794. *On the Song of Songs* (Kalamazoo: Cistercian, 1979) I, p. 16.

[5]*Ibid.*, 9.3: PL 183, 816; Eng. trans. I, p. 55; 12.5, p. 81.

[6]*Ibid.*, 4.1: PL 183, 796–797. Eng. trans. I, p. 21.

[7]Richard of Saint Victor, *De quatuor gradibus violentae caritatis:* PL 196, 1207–1224.

[8]"Strong desires," *Revelations*, I.8. Depression, I.10; "melting heart," I.11; "filled abundantly with the Holy Spirit," I.14.

[9]Gertrude, *Revelations*, I.11. Gertrude had been preceded in her allusions to mystical phenomena by Elizabeth of Schoenau who in her writings distinguished when she was in ecstasy and when she was almost in ecstasy (*Vita*, nn. 30 and 22: PL 195, 136 and 132), and visions seen without being in ecstasy (*Vita*, 27: PL 195, 135), painful ecstasy from ecstasy without suffering (*Vita*, n. 39: PL 195, 141), visions with the eyes of the spirit and visions with the eyes of the body (*Vita*, 26: PL 195.134). But neither Elizabeth nor Gertrude distinguishes successive stages of prayer.

[10]Hadewijch, *The Complete Works* (New York: Paulist, 1980): "God embraced me in my interior senses and took me away in spirit" (vision 3, p. 272; cf. vision 5, p. 276); "my senses were drawn inward with a great tempestuous clamor" (vision 4, p. 273); "I experienced desires and an exceedingly strong longing" (vision 6, p. 278); "my heart and my veins and all my limbs trembled and quivered" (vision 7, p. 280).

[11]J. Ruusbroec, *The Spiritual Spousals* (New York: Paulist, 1985).

[12]Teresa of Jesus, *Spiritual Testimonies*, n. 1, I, p. 311.

[13]Teresa of Jesus, *Int. Castle*, IV, 3.3, II, pp. 328–329.

[14]Teresa of Jesus, *Int. Castle*, IV, 3.4–7, II, p. 329–331.

[15]Teresa of Jesus, *Int. Castle*, IV, 2.3, II, p. 323.

[16]Teresa of Jesus, *Int. Castle*, V, 2.5, II, p. 343.

[17]Teresa of Jesus, *Life*, 18.10, I, p. 120.

[18]Teresa of Jesus, *Int. Castle*, VI, 6.2, I, p. 391.

[19]Teresa of Jesus, *Int. Castle*, VI, 6.3, I, p. 392.

9: *Prayer in the Dark*

[1]Teresa of Jesus, *Int. Castle*, VI, 7, 7, II, p. 400.

[2]Teresa of Jesus, *Way*, 34.12 (61.8). In ICS edition 34.11. II, p. 173.

[3]Teresa of Jesus, *Int. Castle*, 7.9, II, p. 401.

[4]Teresa of Jesus, *Int. Castle*, VII, 3.8, p. 440.

[5]John of the Cross, *Dark Night*, II, 1, pp. 329–330.

[6]A. Royo and J. Aumann, *The Theology of Christian Perfection* (Dubuque: Priory Press, 1962) p. 342.

[7]Teresa of Jesus, *Int. Castle*, VI, 1.7, II, p. 362.

[8]Auguste Poulain, *The Graces of Interior Prayer*, III, ch. 15 (London: Routledge and Kegan, 1950) pp. 215–218.

[9]Teresa of Jesus, *Int. Castle*, VI, 7.2–4, II, pp. 397–399.

[10]Catherine of Genoa, Purgatory 17: *Purgation and Purgatory: The Spiritual Dialogue* (New York: Paulist, 1979) p. 81.

[11]Louis de Blois, O.S.B., *Speculum Spirituale*, ch. 11.

[12]Teresa of Jesus, *Int. Castle*, VII, 4.4–5, p. 445.

[13]Angela of Foligno, *Visions and Instructions*, ch. 64 (Leamington: Art and Book, 1888) p. 303.

[14]Catherine of Genoa, *Dialogue*, II, 10 in *Purgation and Purgatory*, pp. 116–118.

[15]Anna Catherine Emmerich, *The Passion of Our Lord Jesus Christ*, ch. 53 (Clyde: Benedictine Convent of Perpetual Adoration, 1914) pp. 291–292.

10: *You Shall Love the Lord Your God with All Your Heart*

[1]Angela of Foligno, *Visions*, ch. 64.

[2]Cf. a description of the transforming union in *Le Te-*

moignage de Marie de l'Incarnation (Paris: Beauchesne, 1932) pp. 271–275.

[3]Evagrius, *Praktikos*, ch. 3: PG 79, 1168. Eng. trans. by J. E. Bamberger, *The Praktikos, Chapters on Prayer* (Kalamazoo: Cistercian, 1978) p. 16.

[4]Teresa of Jesus, *Int. Castle*, VII, 1.9, II, p. 431.

[5]John Wesley, *A Plain Account of Christian Perfection*, n. 10. In John and Charles Wesley, *Selected Writings and Hymns* (New York: Paulist, 1981) pp. 303–305.

[6]Teresa of Jesus, *Int. Castle*, VII, 1.10, II, pp. 431–432.

[7]*Ibid.* VI, 1.7, II, p. 430.

[8]Gregory of Nyssa, *In Cant. Hom. VI:* PG 44, 888.

[9]*Ibid.* Hom. XI: PG 44, 1000.

[10]Origen, *On Prayer*, 9.2, in *An Exhortation to Martyrdom, Prayer and Selected Writings* (New York: Paulist, 1979) p. 99.

Index of Names of Persons, Movements and Anonymous Works

Abraham of Nathpar, 10

Alacoque, Margaret-Marie, 128

Alexandrian Neoplatonism, 78

Alvarez, Baltasar, 24, 95, 104, 105, 110, 111, 113

Alvarez, Rodrigo, 133

Ambrose of Milan, 34

Angela of Foligno, 147, 152, 158, 160

Anthony, anchorite, 121

Aquinas, Thomas, 50, 106

Augustine of Hippo, 6, 8, 9, 12, 15, 19, 22, 43, 67, 68, 71, 123, 130

Banez, Domingo, 24

Barat, Madeleine Sophie, 61

Benedict of Nursia, 67

Benedictine monasticism, 55, 67

Bernard of Clairvaux, 15, 16, 84, 109, 123, 124, 131, 132

Bernardo de Laredo, 133

Blosius (Louis de Blois), 152

Bonaventure, 82, 106

Borgia, Francis, 114

Buber, Martin, 14

Buddhism, 5, 152, 161, 165

Camara, Helder, 52

Catherine of Genoa, 147, 154

Catherine of Siena, 164, 165

Chantal, Jane Frances de, 80, 127, 149

Cistercians, 165

Claret, Anthony, 43, 60, 61, 69, 153, 164, 165

Clement of Alexandria, 34, 71, 122

Cloud of Unknowing, The, 109

Cyprian of Carthage, 8–9

Desert Fathers and Mothers, 66, 71, 109, 121

Devotio Moderna, 71

Didache, 39

Eckhardt, Meister, 68, 123
Elizabeth of Hungary, 51, 68
Elizabeth, mother of John, 101
Elizabeth of the Trinity, 21, 63, 64, 127
Emmerich, Ann Catherine, 159
Eusebius of Caesarea, 34
Evagrius of Pontus, 6, 12, 14, 15, 19, 20, 47, 162

Fitzgerald, Constance, 91
Flemish-Rhineland mysticism, 68, 71
Foucauld, Charles de, 164
Fowler, James, 62
Francis de Sales, 76, 80, 165
Francis Xavier, 60
Francis of Assisi, 15, 53, 54, 84, 93, 164
Francisco de Osuna, 133

Gertrude the Great, 48, 67, 128, 131
Gonzalez i Puig, Esperanza, 152
Gracian, Jeronimo, 24
Gregory of Nazianz, 67
Gregory of Nyssa, 6, 50, 67, 90, 122, 130, 167
Guzman, Dominic de, 165

Hadewijch, 67, 128, 132
Hassel, David, 45
Hoyos, Bernardo, 128

Ignatius Loyola, 43, 46, 57, 61, 64, 68, 79, 83, 84, 93, 127, 164

d'Igny, Guerric, 64
Illuminati, 79
Isaac of Nineveh, 130
Isidore of Seville, 71
Islam, 161

Jaspers, Karl, 154
Jerome, 6
John the Baptizer, 34
John Bosco, 61
John Cassian, 122
John Climacus, 6
John Damascene, 12
John of God, 51, 68
John of the Cross, 22, 53, 54, 64, 67, 70, 84, 92, 94, 103, 107, 108, 110, 111, 113, 118, 122, 123, 127, 146, 147, 148, 149, 150, 160, 165
Joseph, husband of Mary, 32
Josephus, Flavius, 158
Julian of Norwich, 22
Jung, Carl, 63, 80

King, Martin Luther, 52

Lane, Belden, 91
Lazarus, 101, 102, 103
Letter of Barnabas, 71
Luis de Leon, 82
Luther, Martin, 19, 21, 22

McAuley, 61
Macarius, Pseudo, 122
Marie of the Incarnation, 127, 147–148, 150, 153, 161, 166
Marrilac, Louise de, 51, 60

Mary, Blessed Mother of Jesus, 32, 101, 102, 103, 114, 138
Mary Magdalen, 114
Matel, Jeanne Chezard de, 128–129
Maximus the Confessor, 122
Mechtild of Hackeborn, 67, 128, 131
Mechtild of Magdeburg, 67, 131
Merton, Thomas, 48–49, 56, 128
Monasticism, Christian, 15, 66–67, 71, 82, 109
Monica, 9
Moses, 6, 50, 51
Muslim mystics, 152, 161

Nadal, Jerome, 57, 61
Neoplatonism, 11, 83–84

Origen, 11, 19, 34, 56, 122

Paul the apostle, 66
Paul of the Cross, 150, 153
Peter of Alcantara, 24
Philo of Alexandria, 6, 50
Poulain, Auguste, 147, 148
Pseudo-Dionysius, 84, 122

Quietism, 79

Rahner, Karl, 7, 9
Rhineland mysticism, 68, 123
Richard of Saint Victor, 131

Rodriguez, Alfonso, 79, 118
Romero, archbishop, 50, 52
Ruusbroec, John, 132

Seton, Elizabeth Ann, 94, 127, 128
Simeon the New Theologian, 84
Stein, Edith, 63, 127
Suso, Henry, 68, 123

Tauler, John, 68, 123
Teilhard de Chardin, Pierre, 55
Teresa of Jesus, 14, 15, 23–27, 41, 43, 47–48, 63, 68, 73, 83, 90, 102, 104, 109, 111, 113, 114, 118, 128, 129, 133, 135, 137, 139, 140, 143, 145, 146, 152, 154, 159, 160, 164, 166, 167
Therese de Lisieux, 63, 64
Thomas of Celano (biographer of Francis), 15

Ulloa, Guiomar de, 24

Vincent de Paul, 61, 68, 153, 165

Weil, Simone, 57
Wesley, John, 22, 163
William of Saint Thierry, 13, 71